■ **Bicycling Maga**

Ride Like
a Pro

Bicycling Magazine's
Ride Like a Pro

By the Editors of *Bicycling* Magazine

 Rodale Press, Emmaus, Pennsylvania

Compiled by *Ed Pavelka*

Edited by *Kathleen Becker*

Production editor: *Jane Sherman*

Copy editor: *Lisa D. Andruscavage*

Cover and interior design: *Lisa Farkas*

Book layout: *Peter A. Chiarelli*

Cover photo: *David Madison*

If you have any questions or comments concerning this book, please write:
    Rodale Press
    Book Reader Service
    33 East Minor Street
    Emmaus, PA 18098

Library of Congress Cataloging-in-Publication Data

Bicycling magazine's ride like a pro / by the editors of Bicycling
    magazine.
            p.   cm.
    Includes bibliographical references.
    ISBN 0-87596-102-9 paperback
        1. Cycling—Training.   2. Bicycle racing—Training.
    I. Bicycling.   II. Title: Ride like a pro.
    GV1048.B5 1992
    796.6-dc20   91-45291
                                                                        CIP

Distributed in the book trade by St. Martin's Press

2 4 6 8 10 9 7 5 3 1 paperback

CONTENTS

◻️ INTRODUCTION

As coach Mike Walden says in his year-round cycling program (which concludes this book), "If you're a fast recreational rider—what I call a super tourist—you can use racing skills to make cycling easier and safer. If you're a racer, you use them to go faster and—who knows?—maybe someday become good enough to ride professionally. Whatever you learn will serve you well, no matter what you aspire to."

And that's the objective of this book. In it, you will find recommendations from numerous pro racers, coaches, and other experts about the key elements of high-performance cycling. There's extensive advice on training, bike-handling skills, and riding techniques as well as clear nutritional guidance and the latest findings on aerodynamics. We even take you into the wind tunnel to learn ways to save valuable minutes in time trials and centuries, using simple equipment modifications.

To supplement the text, we've included photos of professionals in action. Study them well, and also use Walden's tips on having yourself videotaped. Once your riding position and technique begin to mirror a pro's, improvements in fitness and skill will come much more easily.

We also invite you to try Walden's four-part program. It has produced scores of world, national, and district champions as well as many accomplished super tourists. It will give purpose to your cycling and help you improve where you need to most. As the weeks go by, you will reach the forefront of fast recreational riders or advance in organized amateur racing. Even though you may not actually aspire to compete as a pro, there's no reason why you can't ride like one.

Ed Pavelka, Editor at Large
Bicycling Magazine

Part One
RIDING POSITION

1 THE FIRST STEP TO POWERFUL RIDING

Riding like a pro begins with the relationship between your body and bike. If you expect to pedal with the strength and skill of the sport's best riders, you must make sure your position matches the proven guidelines that have evolved from bio-mechanical studies and decades of analyzing the setups of top cyclists.

Strength, Power, and Comfort

Use the following instructions to adjust your position, then think about how it feels during your rides. Fine-tune it until you become as comfortable and as efficient as possible. It's okay if your unique position pushes the limits of the recommended ranges noted below, but be careful about exceeding them. These dimensions have proved to be right for riders who make their

The rewards of a correct riding position include strength, power, comfort, and freedom from injury.

living training and racing hours each day. They demand the same things you seek: strength, power, comfort, and freedom from injury.

Caution: If these guidelines require significant changes in your present position, make them in steps. For example, if your saddle must be raised 4 centimeters, move it a centimeter at a time with several rides between. Otherwise, you'll risk straining your muscles and joints.

1) Stem height. The top of the handlebar stem should be about an inch below the top of the saddle. If you can lower it a little farther without discomfort to your upper body or your breathing, do so—it will make your position more aerodynamic.

2) Brake levers. Your wrists should be straight when grasping the levers from the handlebar drops. This is accomplished by positioning the levers so their tips just touch a straightedge extended forward from under the straight portion of the handlebar.

3) Top tube and stem length. Try this simple test: Sit on the saddle and place your hands on the brake hoods. Does the position of the handlebar keep you from easily seeing the front hub? If so, then the combined top tube and stem length is correct.

This is a starting point, and the result should be a comfortable position with your back straight and your arms slightly bent. If your back is bent, the stem and top tube combination may be too short. As you gain experience, you may benefit from a position that is more extended than normal. Switching to a stem extension that is 1 or 2 centimeters longer can aid aerodynamics, enhance your breathing, and straighten your back.

4) Handlebar. The bottom, flat portion of the bar should be level or pointed slightly down toward the rear hub. The handlebar width should equal your shoulder width to keep your chest area unrestricted. This leaves room for comfortable breathing without creating unnecessary wind drag.

5) Saddle height. The distance from the center of the bottom bracket to the top of the saddle should be 0.885 of your inseam length (measured in stocking feet from floor to crotch). While you're pedaling, your knees should be slightly bent at the bottom of the pedal stroke, and, when viewed from behind, your hips should not rock. Raise the saddle 2 or 3 additional millimeters if you have long feet for your height. The saddle should be level or pointed slightly up at the tip. Don't tilt it down, which causes you to slide forward and place additional weight on your arms.

6) Knee-over-pedal. A plumb line dropped from the bony protrusion below your kneecap should bisect the forward pedal's axle when you're seated comfortably with the crankarms horizontal. Adjust this by moving your saddle fore or aft. You may wish to experiment. Placing the saddle 1 to 2 centimeters farther back fosters a powerful pedaling style for climbing or time trialing. Moving it 1 centimeter forward aids spinning and sprinting.

7) Frame. Frame size refers to seat tube length, generally measured from the center of the bottom bracket (crank axle) to the top of the top tube. It should be such that 4 to 5 inches of seatpost are exposed once saddle height is correct. Overall, a smaller frame is desirable for lightness and stiffness. However, don't use such a small one that the top tube is too short or the seatpost must be set past its maximum extension line.

8) Feet. To prevent knee injury, cleats should be adjusted so that the angle of your foot on the pedal is natural. To visualize this, think of your footprints when you walk from a pool—some people's feet angle outward, while others are pigeon-toed. The Rotational Adjustment Device (RAD), which is part of the Fit Kit bicycle-sizing system used by numerous pro bike shops, can help transfer your natural foot position to the bike. Also, the widest part of each foot should be directly over the pedal axle. Be sure toe clips allow at least 5 millimeters of clearance to the tip of your shoes. If they don't, install a larger size or put washers between each clip and the pedal cage.

9) Crankarm length. The trend is toward longer cranks. These improve leverage but may inhibit spinning. In general, if your inseam is less than 29 inches, use 165-millimeter-long crankarms; 29 to 32 inches, 170-millimeter; 32 to 34 inches, 172.5-millimeter; and more than 34 inches, 175-millimeter. (Crankarm length is measured from the center of the fixing bolt to the center of the pedal mounting hole. It's usually marked on the back.)

2 ■ AERODYNAMICS GIVE FAST RESULTS

These are heady times for cycling's product engineers as they try to bend, twist, and stretch man and machine into ever-sleeker positions. Nowhere is this more evident than at the Texas A&M University Low Speed Wind Tunnel in College Station. It has become the gathering place for our sport's scientists, designers, and athletes.

The Texas tunnel is one of the best in the country for cycling because it functions at relatively low speeds (less than 200 mph). The concept of testing a pedaling bike rider makes perfect sense, because most scientists agree that the body represents about two-thirds of total wind drag. Thus, for companies to spend exorbitant amounts of money testing and refining components without considering riding position is akin to buying a Lear Jet before you have your pilot's license. The same goes for you if you're looking for ways to improve your speed; position refinements should be your first priority.

Finding Speed in Your Position

"This is the training program of the future," says John Cobb, who owns the Racing Research bike shop in Shreveport, Louisiana. He and others combine tunnel data with findings in human performance labs to determine ways to reach peak cycling efficiency.

For example, in one Texas A&M tunnel test overseen by Cobb and other engineers, a bike was held by two pairs of specially fabricated arms that protruded through the floor and attached to the fork tips and chainstays. Riders pedaled at a normal cadence (but against no resistance) while a small motor affixed to one fork blade turned the front wheel to simulate actual conditions. By leaving the handlebar binder bolt loose, position could be altered while riding. Aerodynamic drag (in pounds) was recorded by a computer each time a change was made. Wind speed was a constant 30 mph. The platform could also be rotated to test side forces.

Periodically, the 12½-foot-long rotor blade (salvaged from the Enola Gay, the plane that bombed Hiroshima) was halted, allowing scientists to enter the tunnel and, in a flurry of wrenches, change a bar or reverse a seatpost to check its effect.

As a benchmark, riders were first tested in their standard riding positions. Then the handlebar was lowered, the arms brought inward, or the seat moved forward for better aerodynamics. An adjustable stem was used to test extremely low, forward positions.

This test determined that using an aero bar with elbow rests (instead of a standard drop model) lowers drag more than any other modification and typically saves at least a minute in a 40-kilometer time trial, the U.S. championship distance. In fact, by simply using an aero extension bolted to a standard bar, one 32-year-old amateur racer was able to lower his drag of 9.03 pounds to 7.44 pounds. The difference of 1.59 pounds equates to a savings of more than 4 minutes over 40 kilometers.

Other consistently effective changes included lowering the bar and bringing the arms closer together. For the rider just cited, sinking the stem all the way into the steerer (about 1½ inches lower) and rotating the armrests of the bolt-on bar inward (elbows almost touching, rather than 6 inches apart) produced his lowest drag figure. It dropped to 6.75 pounds, worth almost 2 minutes more in a 40-kilometer time trial. No other change—including using a radical forward-saddle position—had as great an effect.

The Aero Debate

Indeed, the extreme forward-saddle position embraced by numerous professional biathletes and triathletes has been cause for lively debate. Some experts have argued against such a major alteration of knee position relative to the bottom bracket, but it became contagious when stars like Ken Souza, Mike Pigg, and Mark Allen adopted the position in 1989. It even spawned specially designed frames with 90-degree seat tubes (radical when compared to the conventional 72- to 74-degree tubes). By using an aero bar and placing the tip of the saddle ahead of the bottom bracket (rather than several centimeters behind, as is customary), the rider gets low and flat, minimizing frontal area. There is a trade-off, though, since it causes a loss of climbing power. It also requires relearning how to pedal. Instead of just pushing down with your quadriceps, this new position requires you to pull up with your hamstrings.

But, as often happens with cycling trends, the pendulum began swinging back quite quickly as triathletes reconsidered the merits of a more conventional setup. Souza, one of the first to return to a standard saddle position, revealed why he tried the radical forward position to begin with. "The only reason I moved was to stay in the saddle. I found myself always on the tip, so I just kept moving it forward." At one point, his saddle tip was 7 centimeters in front of the bottom bracket, but later he returned it to 1 centimeter behind and saw his climbing improve. Even with standard saddle placement, Souza has a drag figure of just 6.12 pounds, perhaps because his back flexibility enables him to remain flat and low. (Greg LeMond, by the way, advocates a rearward position and uses a 72½-degree seat-tube angle to place his saddle well behind the bottom bracket.)

The Experts' Indecision

Indecision by athletes such as Souza reflects a similar lack of consensus within the industry. Cobb, for instance, believes in the forward philosophy enough to have designed a bent seatpost that helps achieve it. Nonetheless, he has expressed reservations about some of the extreme positions being used.

According to Cobb, during hard braking, the rear wheel can leave the ground and make the bike difficult to steer. Some designers have sought to alleviate this by increasing the distance from the bottom bracket to the front axle, known as front-center. For most riders, Cobb recommends a moderate forward position (saddle tip no more than 5 centimeters ahead of the bottom bracket) as a way to improve aerodynamics and power. He says testing has shown a 10 to 15 percent power increase at the same heart rate because the powerful muscles of the thighs and buttocks are working simultaneously.

On the other hand, the designer of Scott USA aero bars, Boone Lennon, is emphatically opposed to a forward position. "I don't believe in it, " he says, and he uses examples of the world's top pros to make his point. Lennon claims that putting such a large proportion of weight on the front wheel could make it fail or cause an unskilled rider to lose control.

Lennon also notes that road racers such as LeMond and Sean Yates simply bolted on aero bars and were immediately able to achieve a low, flat position without moving their seats forward. "Look at the pros," he says. "All those miles have to be worth something. These guys have a flat back because they've trained themselves to sit 'in' the bike and rotate their hips forward.

LeMond says [using an aero bar] hasn't changed the way he pedals."

Wind-tunnel testing hasn't done much to quell these arguments. In fact, some riders record greater drag when trying a forward-bent seatpost and very low bar (instead of simply using a bolt-on aero bar), while others show the opposite. The key element appears to be whether the move forward flattens the back.

Other Sources of Drag

How can reaching for your water bottle or shifting gears affect your aerodynamics? These simple maneuvers were also put to the test, and the results were surprising. Wind-tunnel research shows that reaching down to do either can increase your drag by about 1.25 pounds, and doing so ten times can cost you 45 seconds in a 40-kilometer time trial. In addition, placing water bottles on the down and seat tubes can be costly in a crosswind, creating almost 2 extra pounds of drag and costing you as much as 90 seconds over 40 kilometers. To reduce drag significantly, mount your water bottle behind the seat or use a water carrier that straps to your back.

In another test, Race Across America competitor Dave Bogdan wore wool tights and a loose-fitting rain jacket in the tunnel. Drag increased from 7.63 to 9.27 pounds, equal to about 4 minutes over 40 kilometers. Cobb attributed most of this to the jacket, since previous tests had shown tights to have a negligible effect. Therefore, wearing such a jacket could cost you half an hour during a day-long ride.

Everyone Can Benefit from Aerodynamics

Where is all this aerodynamic innovation leading? Cobb and Lennon agree that the ultimate beneficiary will be recreational riders, not just pro athletes. Anytime you're riding faster than about 15 mph, the bulk of your effort goes toward fighting an invisible foe—the wind. Thus, an aero bar (and other types of wind-cheating modifications) can benefit anyone. By simply using a bolt-on model, you may find that your speed increases 1 to 2 mph. In addition, your comfort improves because your upper-

Going faster means getting lower, which is the best position for cutting wind resistance.

body weight is supported by your arms' bone structure rather than your muscles and joints.

As Cobb notes, "When I show tourists this stuff in my shop, they say, 'Maybe I shouldn't be here.' But then I say, 'You need this more than anyone.'"

How to Become a Bullet

Cobb and Lennon have worked in the wind tunnel enough to know which changes have the greatest aerodynamic benefit. However, because air resistance is dependent on rider size as well as the interaction of bike and body, it's difficult to make a foolproof position prescription. For instance, angling a bolt-on bar upward may decrease drag for you, but maybe the reverse is true for someone else.

"We can easily say that any aero bar is better," says Cobb. "We can also say that the flatter your back and the narrower your elbows, the more aerodynamic you'll be. These are the blanket statements that can be made."

Follow These Aero Axioms

First, get narrow. Next, get flat.

"Narrowness pays off in spades," says Lennon. "The more your elbows come in, the faster you'll go." Putting theory into practice, bolt-on aero bars began coming with adjustable armrests in 1991, allowing riders to position them as close as comfort allowed.

As for getting flat, Lennon suggests using the simplest form of biofeedback—look in the mirror. "Put your bike on a stationary trainer and lean on your regular bar with your elbows and see if there is a hump in your back. If so, you need to change something."

What to change, however, is controversial. Lennon recommends either altering your bar height or conditioning your body to rotate the hips, almost as if you're trying to make your navel touch the top tube. "You have to get down into the bike," he emphasizes. "Separate your elbows and your butt."

Others advocate moving forward with the aid of a steep-seat-tube bike or by reversing your seatpost. This prevents a low, narrow position from inhibiting your breathing or causing your knees to strike your chest. To keep the same thigh/torso angle as with a conventional position, you must move the seat forward or choose a frame that is designed to (in effect) move the bottom bracket back.

To attain a good aero position, you'll probably need to combine these approaches. Move your saddle forward slightly (enough to retain free breathing while preventing the knees from hitting the chest), and strive to achieve a flat back by rotating your hips. A forward seat position may also improve comfort if you consistently find yourself riding on the saddle tip during hard efforts.

Keep in mind, however, that moving forward may result in a loss of climbing power when seated. Also, you'll need to extend your reach at least an equal amount by purchasing a longer stem or a full or bolt-on aero bar. (If you move your saddle forward 4 centimeters, move your hands forward that much or more.) To alleviate pressure on the crotch in a forward position, tip the saddle down *slightly*. Cobb calls this sitting in the "cradle" of the bike, with a low, flat torso supported at each end by the butt and elbows.

Choose the Right Aero Bar Angle

It's impossible to prescribe an exact aero bar angle, although wind-tunnel testing has shown that it shouldn't point below horizontal or higher than about 30 degrees. Lennon terms it a comfort option. Overall, he says, "Try to keep your chin down behind your hands or you'll create a cup that catches wind. Train to keep your head down." Again, the mirror can be a valuable aid. View yourself from the front, and concentrate on presenting as little area as possible.

Don't expect to achieve the perfect position immediately. For instance, get narrower by degrees, gradually moving the arms inward as you gain flexibility and bike-handling confidence. Then, when comfortable, lower your stem to decrease frontal area and attain a flat back.

Aero-Handling Techniques

Besides getting used to your new body position after installing a full or bolt-on aero bar, you'll need to relearn how to handle your bike. The steering is much more sensitive, so oversteering is a common problem. Mostly, this is because you're using the larger muscles of your torso and shoulders, rather than just your hands and arms. (Bikes designed specifically for aero bars have slower front ends and increased front-center distances to alleviate this.)

To ease your transition, start with a moderate position (stem high, arms wide for leverage) and get lower and narrower by degrees. For fast descents, bumpy sections, and tight corners, move to a higher leverage position by placing your hands on the wider portion of a full aero bar or by moving from a bolt-on to your conventional bar. Do the same for steep climbs to allow free breathing. As you develop a feel for the new low position, you'll be able to stay there longer.

As with a regular bar, avoid a death grip. Because of the increased sensitivity, even small bumps, when transmitted through rigid arms, can cause the bike to veer dangerously. Come off the aero bar to shift or drink, or do these on smooth pavement only. Slight head movements can cause you to swerve, too, so sit up when looking to the rear or mount a mirror on your helmet or handlebar.

Also, always look well down the road for hazards. Don't let your low head position cause you to become transfixed on the pavement directly ahead. Most full bars and all bolt-ons don't allow for braking when in a full tuck. Consequently, use a conventional position in traffic. Also, it's bad etiquette to be without brakes in a paceline, so adopt your aero position only when taking a pull at the front. The other riders will appreciate it.

Part Two

TECHNIQUES FROM THE PROS

3 ALEXI GREWAL ON SEATED CLIMBING

Alexi Grewal is as well-known for his climbing ability as he is for his tempestuous disposition. Often, the two coincide—and the sight of the 1984 Olympic road champ angrily stomping the pedals up a mountain is unforgettable. Grewal showed his prowess in 1990 by winning the famed Bob Cook Memorial Hill Climb, the 28-mile ascent of Colorado's 14,264-foot Mount Evans, shown in the photo on page 18. He finished in 1:46:29, averaging a record 15.8 mph. In this chapter Grewal shares his successful climbing technique.

Climbing in the Saddle

On Mount Evans I sat 98 percent of the time. Even in the Tour de France, riders sit better than 90 percent. If the grade is

Road champ Alexi Grewal on his way to winning the 1990 Bob Cook Memorial Hill Climb.

steady and not too steep you don't need to get out of the saddle. You should stand in a slightly bigger gear and use your whole body to get over a steep pitch, or to change position and relax. But as soon as you stand, you involve the rest of your body and your caloric needs and heart rate go up.

Choosing a Saddle Height

During the last five years I've moved very far forward and up. I set my saddle as high as I can without sacrificing a smooth pedal stroke. I've had difficulty getting power from my hips, so I've tried to increase the angle between my femur (thighbone) and upper body. The leg has the most power in the middle of its range of motion. For me, sitting back in the traditional saddle position created too sharp an angle at the hip. Particularly if you're long and lean, you can't be folding your body up.

The feet play an important role, too. Some riders pedal with their toes down and some with their heels down. I pedal toes down, so relative to someone who doesn't, I can sit much higher. When your foot is horizontal at the bottom of the pedal stroke, you should have 13 degrees of angle behind your knee. This should about equal the angle between the femur and upper body.

Moving the Saddle Fore or Aft

I'm 6-feet-2 and have a long femur, yet I sit far forward. The tip of my saddle is 1 centimeter behind the bottom bracket. This is the most efficient position for getting power from my hips. But a lot depends on what you're comfortable with. Greg LeMond generates plenty of power with his seat back. The goal is to use your quadriceps and hamstrings. Generally, when you sit farther forward, you get more out of your hamstrings.

Pedaling Technique

For seated climbing, especially if you're pushing a big gear, you should try to generate equal power on the downstroke and upstroke. I don't pull back like many people recommend. I just push down and pull up, while trying to eliminate any dead period at the bottom. The hamstrings and psoas muscles (back of the thigh/lower back) are used when pulling up. The psoas are your most powerful muscles pound for pound, except for the jaw. But they have a limited range of effective power, and you must position yourself so they can work. When you open up the angle between your femur and upper body, you get much more power from them.

Gearing and Cadence

I use 42/53-tooth chainrings. But in the Tour, I would use a 39T inner ring and a tighter freewheel for better shifting. In the United States, a 39 isn't necessary. A 42 × 21T low gear covers almost everything for me. The smallest gear I used on Mount Evans was 42 × 16.

I use as big a gear as possible. I don't like to climb at a high cadence. However, sometimes you're forced to pedal faster to save your legs. In the beginning of a race, for instance, it's important to conserve your legs with a higher cadence and use your heart rate more. But the higher your cadence, the more oxygen you consume. You don't want to pedal faster to save your legs and go into oxygen debt as a result. It takes a long time to learn the limits of leg versus aerobic power.

Breathing

Your natural rhythm is best. The key is to learn not to break out of it. Breathe measured breaths and don't panic—you can ride above yourself if you stay in control. If you're panting, you may not be getting as much oxygen as you were when your heart was five beats per minute slower. There are tricks, too. If you breathe a lot at the bottom of the climb, you can overcharge your system with oxygen. Or try taking one or two deep breaths and not exhaling immediately. Hold it for a second. A lot of riders do this unconsciously after cresting a climb. Also, you can listen to other riders' breathing and tell if they're at their redline. If their breathing is even, they have something in reserve.

Upper Body

I don't concentrate on relaxing or being still. Some guys never rock, but I do. It's just the way I ride. You don't want to be fighting yourself, but at the same time your upper body and arms are stabilizing points.

Hand Position

Use two or three different grips to climb with, including holding the brake hoods with the fingers closed, resting on top of the hoods with the fingers open, or grasping the handlebar tops. Don't get stuck in one mode.

◼ 4 DAVIS PHINNEY ON OUT-OF-SADDLE CLIMBING

By his own admission, Davis Phinney is not a born climber. His solid, 5-foot-9, 160-pound frame is best suited to sprinting, as evidenced by his two Tour de France and 22 Coors Classic stage victories. Nonetheless, Phinney has worked hard at climbing better, and it paid off in 1988 when he won the mountainous Coors Classic. In these next few pages, Phinney tells us what made the difference.

When to Stand

There are two reasons to stand: To attain a more powerful position and to alleviate fatigue in your legs. If the hill is short, I'll just pop out of the saddle. But on a long climb, I'll sit until my legs fatigue, then stand for short periods. You must go totally by feel. It depends on what gear you're using and the pace you're trying to hold. If the pace is high, you must get out of the saddle regularly—every few minutes, or every 30 seconds on steep climbs. On grades of 3 to 6 percent I don't stand much, but on those of 7 to 12 percent I do it more. On the Devil's Kitchen (a 15-percent grade in the Tour de Trump) I was out of the saddle almost the whole time. (See the photo on page 22.)

Davis Phinney demonstrates the right position for out-of-saddle climbing.

How Long to Stand

Generally, you don't want to be out of the saddle for a long time because you consume additional oxygen. You're using your arms and upper body more. But it depends on how tired you are. On a long climb I'll stand for 20 seconds to a minute. If I'm really tired, I may stand for 5 minutes because it's the only way to get power to the pedals. When I'm really strong, such as after a major tour, I tend to sit longer.

Shifting

On long climbs I shift up one gear to stand, then shift back down to sit. The key is to maintain speed. A lot of people equate standing with sprinting. They stand and spin out. It's better to shift up a gear. However, in rolling terrain I'll stand without shifting and try to maintain a comfortable cadence.

Rocking the Bike

There are two extremes. Some people hold their bikes and bodies rigid, while others with weak upper bodies snake and weave up the hill, making S curves. Don't do either. You should gently move the bike side to side 6 to 10 inches at the handlebar. However, be sure to direct your energy into going forward and keep the wheels straight.

Relaxing

When you're out of the saddle, your heart rate will increase. This is why it's important to relax—shoulders, arms, the entire upper body. It's not like sprinting, where you use all your muscles. Alternate pulling on the handlebar with one arm while relaxing the other. I even recommend opening up that hand as practice, to develop a tension/release rhythm. The bike is stable, so you won't lose your grip.

Using Body Weight

I'm a heavy rider—a classic mesomorph. In fact, I weigh 20 pounds more than (teammate) Andy Hampsten, even though we're the same height. He's smooth and spends a lot of time in the saddle. Because I'm heavier, my quadriceps aren't always powerful enough, so I need the strength in my arms and back to help me climb. Even though standing has a cardiovascular cost, I just don't have the strength in my legs to sit and power my weight over climbs.

I try to place the bulk of my weight over the pedals where it will have the greatest effect. The back of my thighs are just in front of the seat. But it depends on the fit of your bike. You must have the right top tube and stem lengths. Sometimes a rearward weight shift is beneficial. If it's wet, sandy, or steep, you have to bend more severely and get your weight back. It's sort of sitting and standing at the same time.

Hand Position

Keep your hands on the brake hoods. On climbs you're not interested in being aero. You want to get as much air as you can into your lungs. Stay upright with your chest open. Use the drops only if you're sprinting over a small hill.

Upper Body Position

I often see people who are much too rigid. There's no natural sway. You should develop a side-to-side motion where one arm pulls up while the opposite leg pushes down. Also, keep your shoulders and hips square. Your head shouldn't dip, even though you're rocking the bike.

Pedaling

Some people who pedal smoothly when seated are jerky when they stand. It's hard to have a completely round stroke, but it's important to at least think about pushing down and pulling up. People tend to snap their legs straight, and that puts a dead spot in the stroke. Make your legs 95 percent straight at the bottom of the stroke, but not 100 percent. Andy Hampsten pedals exactly the same standing or sitting. It takes practice. Emulate the pro riders and think about what you're doing. That's the key to efficiency.

Training

Climbing is a function of weight, cardiovascular condition, and power. Because I'll always be heavier than a climbing specialist, I have to work on cardiovascular fitness and power. I train to be able to maintain my heart rate at a high level without blowing up. I do this by going to my anaerobic threshold and holding it for 20 minutes at a time. My performance also depends on the gradient. In the Coors Classic it was rarely more than 8 percent, but in the Tour de Trump and Tour de France the hills were 12 to 14 percent. At that point I can't maintain my momentum. There's no way I can carry my 20 extra pounds uphill faster than Andy Hampsten or Greg LeMond. I can improve it with training, but I'll never be as fast because of the weight difference.

Maintaining Pedal Pressure

When standing in a group, don't drop-kick the guy behind you. It's common for unskilled riders to stand and move back 6 inches relative to the rider behind. As you rise out of the saddle, do it with a smooth, even pedal stroke so as not to lose speed.

5 STEVE BAUER ON FULL-TUCK DESCENDING

Since winning an Olympic silver medal in 1984, Canadian Steve Bauer has become one of the most successful Europe-based pros. In 1990 he wore the yellow leader's jersey in the Tour de France for ten days and finished second in the Paris-Roubaix classic. Bauer describes his full-tuck technique.

The Best Time to Tuck

Usually you only tuck if you have the time and space—for instance, if you're alone and in the wind. You have to have the time to get down and make it worthwhile. In some mountainous stages of the Tour de France, you can't do it. It's so fast that you don't need to get aero—you need to keep your head up and your eyes open because anything can happen. Also, when you're in a pack of riders and following a wheel, you don't need aerodynamics. You need to be stable and alert.

Body and Hand Position

Basically, you need to get everything tight to reduce frontal area. Keep your chest out of the wind, your knees and elbows in, and your head low. If it's a straight shot, you can reach a much higher speed by putting the front of your shoulders—your deltoids—right on the bar. But this can be dangerous because your weight is so far forward.

Some riders like to put their hands on the bar tops, but if you're already pushing for top speed, you can lose a lot of stability that way. It's faster but riskier. It's crazy to do it if the road is rough. You're less likely to fall with your hands on the drops, and you can brake.

Fore/Aft Balance

If it's rough, I move back in the saddle, but I still try to get low. When you're farther forward over the front wheel, you're not as stable. Your balance and control aren't as good.

Vision

Try to keep your head up—not 100 percent of the time, but at least enough to know what's in front. It's like driving a car. You don't want to look directly ahead, but you want to focus down the road. I follow objects, too—you might see a hole or obstacle and watch it come closer to make sure you avoid it. If something looks dangerous, you might have to jump your bike. Bring your chest up and level the pedals so you can spring with your arms and legs.

Headwear and Clothing

In a road race, you wear a helmet for safety—you're not so much concerned about its aero benefits. That's more of an issue in time trials. Glasses are a plus for flying stones, bugs, and wind. They're not a must, but they can be a big safety factor. The fastest

Olympic medalist Steve Bauer tucked in tight, speeding downhill.

we go in the Tour is about 62 mph. Small chips flying at that speed can be dangerous.

If there's a big change in temperature as you're climbing, it's a good idea to grab some newspaper or plastic and stuff it under your jersey for the descent. If it's cold or raining, you must put on a jacket. Climb without it, then put it on for the downhill. The longer the descent, the more it's an advantage to be warm.

Gearing and Braking

My biggest gear is 53 × 12-tooth. It's rare to use a larger one in a road race, although I will in a time trial.

The front brake is the most powerful, and you can use it positively if the road is good and dry. Otherwise, in varying conditions, use the front and rear.

6 FRANKIE ANDREU ON PACK RIDING

To a large degree, being comfortable in a pack of riders, whether it's a race or recreational event, depends on how much time you've spent in one—and this makes Frankie Andreu an authority on the subject. He began racing at age 8, won five national championships, and turned pro in 1989. Here's Andreu's advice for making the most of pack riding.

Position in the Pack

With a big field, you need to stay among the first 10 or 15 riders. This way you're less likely to crash, and you can pick your line through corners. You'll also expend a lot less energy because every time the pack corners, there's a whiplash effect—those toward the rear are forced to slow, then accelerate. If there are 120 riders, it can take 100 meters to get back to speed. In fact, if you rode at the back the entire race, you might not finish. It's 10 times harder than being in front where you can do your own thing and be aggressive.

Cornering

One of the biggest breaches of etiquette occurs when lining up for a corner. It never fails—someone tries to slam through inside next to the curb. Then words are exchanged, or someone crashes. Once you learn who does this, avoid them. In general, you should follow the same smooth line as everyone. Start wide and cut to the apex.

Concentration

This is crucial. Always be concentrating—not just on what's around you, but on what's happening five or six places in front. When you daydream, you can touch wheels and crash.

Riding Position

When I'm in the middle of the pack, I mostly ride on the hoods. I stay relaxed and try not to burn a lot of nervous energy. When I'm close to the front, I ride on the drops more. This way I'm more aerodynamic and ready to respond to attacks.

Dealing with Wind

If it's a headwind, you can just sit in and relax. But if it's a crosswind, you should be in the top five because this is where the race is won or lost. The field will break up into echelons (staggered pacelines) as each rider tries to get into the slipstream that occurs to the left or right, depending on wind direction, of the rider ahead. If you're near the front, you'll make the first echelon and possibly escape.

Avoiding Crashes

The most common cause of a pileup is trying to go through a hole that isn't there. Then you hit handlebars and crash. You should realize that if you're in the middle of a race, shooting for one gap won't make any difference. Also, if you hear a crash behind, don't look back. It's tempting to want to see what happened, but you may swerve and crash yourself or take someone else down.

I reach ahead and tap people on the hip a fair amount just to say, "Hey, I'm here," particularly when entering a corner. However, sometimes you have to yell. If you're pinned against the curb and someone moves over, you might crash. So shout if you need to.

Physical Contact, Overlapping Wheels

Occasionally, you'll bump elbows as someone moves over on you. This shouldn't be a problem. The main thing is to be relaxed. Keep your elbows bent and absorb the shock with your arms.

If you're going straight, it's okay to overlap the wheel ahead a little, but if you're entering a corner you should be behind it. Otherwise, if the person ahead changes his line, he could hit your wheel and take you down.

Braking

Occasionally, someone will lock up the brakes and cause a problem. I always try to slow gradually. Also, I tend to use the rear brake more in a pack. With the front, there's a chance of stopping too quickly or going over the bar.

Climbing and Descending

Even if you're a good climber, you should move to the front for big hills. This way, if you're climbing with the leaders and you tire, you can drift back and still be with the bunch. Also, something a lot of riders don't realize is that when you rise out of the saddle, you have to maintain pressure on the pedals. Otherwise, you'll cause the bike to slow and go backward several inches relative to the rider behind, hitting his wheel. A lot of crashes happen this way.

When descending, the closer you are to the front, the safer you'll be. Keep at least a bike length between you and the person ahead. This way you can judge what you need to do for the next corner by watching that rider. I hardly ever lead. I let the other guy go as fast as possible.

Attacking

If you're going to attack, it's best to do it from about the 10th position. Don't jump from 30th place because everyone will see you coming. I also like to wait for the tempo to pick up, which causes the group to ride single file. In any case, you have to be toward the front. Position is crucial.

7 BRIAN WALTON ON PACELINE RIDING

Brian Walton doesn't need anyone's help to go fast. He excels in individual time trials and was third in the prestigious Grand Prix Eddy Merckx Time Trial in Belgium in 1990. He also won the 1989 British Milk Race, largely due to a crucial time trial victory. Walton also knows plenty about the community of speed called the paceline, and in this chapter he shares with us his tips for participating in a safe, yet powerful, paceline.

Taking the Lead

Don't accelerate too much when you reach the front. It's important to have a cyclecomputer and use it to maintain a steady speed. Remember that it's a team effort.

Length of Pull

In training or during moderate-pace rides, it's okay to pull for several minutes or until speed drops. But you should complete only about 30 pedal revolutions when giving your all in a breakaway or riding in a team time trial. Switch positions quickly to keep the speed high. But it depends on how you feel. Initially in a breakaway, you have to put effort into getting away. Then you can analyze the situation and decide how much work to do. At most, ride 30 seconds to a minute, or until you've passed two telephone poles.

Brian Walton pulls his teammates during a pro race in the Netherlands.

When climbing, finish your pull at either the base or the top of a hill. Generally, on small rollers stay seated to keep things smooth.

Dropping Back and Resting

Remember that your pull doesn't end until you get to the back. Many riders make the mistake of easing up on the pedals too much, drifting quickly to the rear of the group, then sprinting to get back on. This wastes energy.

Sometimes you need a break. When you're at the back you can stand and stretch. This is also the best time to drink or eat.

A word about aero bars here: Riding on an aero bar can be dangerous in a paceline because your hands are too far from the brakes. If you're using one, don't drop onto it before you reach the second position.

Getting into Position

Ride as close to the rider ahead as you feel comfortable. A few inches is ideal, but a foot may be more realistic for most riders. But whatever you do, don't move back and forth and create a yo-yo effect. You need to ride closely, but you can't always be getting too close and braking. Don't look at the wheel of the rider in front. Look at his back.

We always communicate hazards such as medians and potholes. Also, when at the front, you need to make it obvious that you're pulling off. If there are two of you, use a quick hand signal. With more people, pull to the side quickly and deliberately so the others know you're switching. Always check for traffic first.

Reading a Crosswind

If traffic conditions allow, let the wind dictate the direction of the rotation. Try to find shelter. Notice which side of the paceline you feel most comfortable on. You can determine wind direction by looking at a flag, tree, or tall grass.

Standing

If you must get out of the saddle, be careful not to throw your bike backward and bump wheels with the rider behind. This is especially a danger when you're tired. You have to keep pedaling and almost throw your bike forward as you stand.

Shifting

To conserve energy, shift to a lower gear when you get to the rear, then change to a higher one when you reach the second position. This way, you can tell if you're in the right gear to take a pull. You don't want to bog down at the front.

Overlapping Wheels

With two people, or if you're riding in a group you know well, you can usually "half-wheel" the rider ahead. Advance on the leeward side until your tire reaches that rider's rear hub. But beware: If you do this behind someone who's inexperienced in a paceline, there's more danger of a swerve and a crash.

8 RON KIEFEL ON TIME TRIALING

Ron Kiefel has been a member of the 7-Eleven pro team (which became Motorola in 1991) since 1982. He's finished five Tours de France and won a bronze medal in the team time trial at the 1984 Olympics. Entering the 1991 season, he was the third-highest ranked American in international pro cycling behind Greg LeMond and Andy Hampsten. Here are Kiefel's tips for successful time trialing.

Pedaling Technique

Keep your leg speed high. With a high cadence, if you hit a rise, you tend to keep your speed better. Mine is usually 80 to 90 rpm, but some riders on our team push bigger gears with a slower cadence. LeMond is a big-gear stomper. Since I'm not so powerful, I have to compensate by spinning. In long time trials, though, it's hard to keep my cadence high. Maybe that's why I tend to do well in prologues, which are usually less than 5 miles long. But overall, if you spin, you tend to go faster. The Soviet, Viacheslav Ekimov, pedals incredibly fast. His legs go like a sewing machine.

Saddle Position

I set my position with the front of my forward kneecap over the pedal axle or 1 centimeter behind it (when the crankarms are horizontal), and I don't change this for a time trial. In a time trial, I tend to sit forward. Most riders do. Then you move back on a hill for better power.

Power Delivery

Eddie Borysewicz (1984 Olympic coach) taught me how to rest my legs even when going hard. Sometimes you can punch a few strokes on one side and then the other—or apply more power on every third or fourth stroke. Or you can do a hard left every other stroke, and a hard right every other.

Heart Rate

I find my anaerobic threshold and keep it here. Mine is 162 beats per minute, and my maximum is about 173, which is low. Teammate Jeff Pierce, on the other hand, isn't riding his bike unless he's doing 186. It varies, and you have to find your own. A monitor will also confirm how you feel. Sometimes, no matter how hard you pedal, you can't get your heart rate up—your body just won't let you do it. Also, if you're a slow starter, a monitor helps you get up to the proper level of effort faster.

Body Position

Here's a part-by-part rundown on achieving the best body position.

Back. It's best to have a position that results in a flat back, even though I've never been able to achieve one.

Head. Unlike the photo on page 36, which was taken on a closed race course, for safety you must keep your head up and

Fast cadence and good body position are the hallmarks of Ron Kiefel's time trialing style.

your eyes on the road. Glance down only occasionally to check your computer.

Hands. Again, the picture isn't perfect—with an aero bar you want your hands in front of your face for better aerodynamics. But you need a compromise. With my hands way up, my upper arms cramp, and with them down I can breathe more freely. I need to bring my elbows up and out to help me breathe. Also, I've begun using taller posts under the arm supports because they improve comfort.

Upper body. Stay as relaxed as you can unless you need to use your arms to pull up a hill. Beware of expending energy in your upper body.

Tire Pressure

In Europe, the roads are often rough and covered with gravel. We run 125 to 132 psi in back and 120 psi in front. For normal road riding we use 105 psi in front and rear. With a disk wheel you have to be careful, though. If the road is rough and you use a very high tire pressure, you could splinter the wheel. Andy Hampsten did that in the warm-up for a team time trial at the Tour de France.

Clothing

An aero helmet makes a difference, but sometimes it's too hot to use one. Then I figure I might lose some time without it, but at least I won't overheat or blow up. That's a decision I can make as a pro. (Amateurs are required to wear helmets in competition.) Also, when I first went to Europe, I was surprised at everyone riding in skinsuits in all weather. But now I wear one even when it's 45° and just apply oil to my legs. The effort expended in a time trial keeps me warm. In cool weather, wear tights and a jacket to the start, then discard them.

Cyclecomputer

I often use a cyclecomputer and a heart rate monitor. The computer is valuable because it tells how far you have to go. Also, if your speed varies a lot, you're probably not riding that well. It can also help you with gear selection. For instance, sometimes I have noticed that I'm faster in a slightly lower gear—say a 53 × 14 rather than a 53 × 13.

9 CHRIS KOSTMAN ON LONG-DISTANCE CYCLING

One of the great rewards of cycling is being able to ride farther and faster each season. You may remember when 25 miles seemed an insurmountable distance, but it probably wasn't long before you were considering your first century. If you've now reached the point where you can ride a brisk 100-miler, it's time to increase the challenge. Next is the double metric (124 miles), and then comes the event that proves you've arrived as a long-distance cyclist, the double century—200 miles in one day.

Chris Kostman has completed numerous 200-milers, as well as triple and quadruple centuries. His passion for distance led him to do the 200-mile Iditabike mountain bike race in Alaska and two Race Across America qualifiers (700 and 550 miles). In 1987, he completed Race Across America (RAAM)—3,129 miles—in ten days, 23 hours, and 58 minutes. At age 20, he was the youngest rider to ever finish the race. Here, Kostman writes about the secrets of his success.

Double Century: More Than Just Two Centuries

A double century isn't just two consecutive centuries. It's a unique event that requires a different strategy and more careful preparation. Fatigue is a major factor, and proper nutrition is crucial. Conditions vary more—you may start in sunshine and finish 12 hours later in darkness and rain. You'll find parts of the ride painful and battle desires to quit. You'll probably consume 20 bottles of liquid and more than 6,000 calories. But you'll also have the satisfaction of extending the limits of your mind and body, and joining a select group of cyclists who have "done a double."

I use double centuries to gauge my fitness level. Since my difficult but rewarding first double, completed in 14½ hours, I've lowered my time to 9:17. It took years of training, racing, and experimentation to enable me to cover 200 miles so quickly and efficiently. Here are some of the things I learned, which hold true for all long-distance rides.

A Word on Conditioning

Because a double century requires long hours in the saddle, it's important to be comfortable on your bike and have an efficient pedaling style. Follow the advice in chapter 1 or consult with a bike shop that uses the Fit Kit or a similar bicycle-sizing system to ensure that your riding position is correct and your cleats are properly adjusted. If changes are required, give yourself time to adapt.

As you train, concentrate on form. Maintain a brisk cadence (90 to 100 pedal rpm). If possible, have an experienced rider critique your pedaling style, or videotape yourself. You should pedal in smooth circles, and your knees should move vertically in one plane. Riding rollers is an excellent way to improve form.

Ride at least five days each week, gradually increasing intensity and mileage. Keep a training log, noting distance, time, average speed, and terrain. Also record what you eat, how you feel, weight, and resting heart rate. The latter (taken before rising each morning) is an excellent fitness indicator that can alert you to overtraining. When I'm stressed or at my lowest fitness level, my heart zooms along at 55 beats per minute. When I'm at peak fitness it dips to 38 or lower.

A Program to Prepare for "The Double"

Your weekly program should vary in terrain and distance. Few double centuries are flat, so include one or two days of climbing. Do a fast-paced club ride once a week to increase your speed and improve your group riding skills. Maintain this program for at least six weeks.

A Weekly Schedule

Here's an example of a good, basic weekly schedule.

Saturday and Sunday: Long, high-intensity rides, 60 to 80 miles per day.

Monday: Easy spin, 15 to 25 miles.

Tuesday: Rest.

Wednesday through Friday: Gradually increase mileage and intensity, doing 30 to 60 miles per day. For variety try off-road riding, racing, or a triathlon. This is important, because if training gets boring it will also become less intense and less frequent.

Cross-training also enhances overall fitness, which is vital to fighting fatigue in long events. My weekly schedule often includes running, hiking, weight lifting, tae kwon do, racquetball, and ultimate Frisbee. I'm convinced that these activities help my riding. Stretching also helps fight fatigue and prevents cramping. But an athlete's body needs rest, too, so do nothing strenuous at least one day each week.

Stay Focused and Alert

Throughout your preparation, keep your goal in mind and visualize yourself achieving it. Cycling performance is 50 percent mental. It's determination that will see you through your training and enable you to cross the finish line.

Gauge your fitness as the day of the double approaches. Try to comfortably complete a double metric or ride back-to-back centuries one weekend. Ideally, you should do this with two weeks to go. Your time in this test will give you a rough idea of how to pace yourself in the double century.

You're not likely to improve much in the last few days, so don't overdo it in training. Also, now is the time to make sure your bike is working properly. It would be unfortunate not to finish because of a mechanical problem, so have questionable parts replaced.

Nutrition is vital during the last week. Load up on carbohydrate and fluid. I drink a gallon of water on each of these crucial days. Try to get enough sleep, particularly two nights before the event.

The Day of the Ride

Allow plenty of time to travel to the start and register. (Pre-register, if possible.) Stay in a hotel the night before if the event is far from home. Eat a small, simple breakfast, and have a snack about 30 minutes before the start. Then stop eating or it may upset your stomach.

Leave yourself enough time to stretch and loosen up. I prefer not to ride too much beforehand for fear of colliding with another distracted rider. Instead, use the first few miles of the event as your warm-up. Finally, check your equipment to be sure you're fully prepared.

Carry the Right Tools

I recommend carrying a small tool kit, two spare tubes, patch kit, folding tire, two or three large water bottles, emergency food such as an energy bar, cyclecomputer or watch, sunscreen and medical supplies, identification, money, and a route sheet. If you anticipate riding in darkness, take a high-quality cycling light and a reflective vest or ankle bands. Besides your normal cycling clothing and helmet, take sunglasses, arm and leg warmers, and a water-resistant windbreaker.

Taking Off at the Start

Some events are mass-start, while others allow you to begin when you please. In a mass-start don't bother trying to get to the front. It's too congested and dangerous. Be careful when the riders roll out—accidents often occur here.

During the first 10 miles stay off the large chainring. Once you're warm, try joining a paceline of smooth, safe riders traveling at a speed that doesn't make you labor. This will help you go faster as well as provide company. Don't overlap wheels with other riders, and stay away from those who seem unsteady. Eventually, you'll find a group that suits you.

Eat and Drink Enough

As the miles pass, the important things to keep in mind are nutrition, hydration, comfort, and pace. Try to consume 300 calories per hour. (A piece of fruit, for example, has roughly 100 calories. A bran muffin has 150.) Obey the adage that you should drink before you're thirsty and eat before you're hungry.

Many riders consume a combination of fruit, cookies, muffins, and granola bars. However, keeping your energy stores high with these foods requires a lot of eating. You may also find your energy level varies considerably on such a sugary diet. To avoid these problems, I use commercially available carbohydrate drinks. They're a well-balanced source of energy that the body can utilize quickly. If you choose a liquids-only diet, it's imperative that you have experience with it prior to the event to avoid possible digestive problems. I also drink one bottle of water per hour in addition to my liquid food. This is a lot of drinking, but it's necessary for sufficient hydration. Other drinks should not be substituted for plain water.

Stay Comfortable

Staying comfortable depends on other factors, too. Keep spinning. Get out of the saddle frequently to stretch your back. When you do stand, shift to a higher gear to maintain your speed. Well-padded gloves are helpful in fighting numbness, as is changing hand positions frequently. Shoes with hook-and-loop closures allow you to adjust the pressure on your feet while riding. Insoles or orthotics help avoid numbness and "hot foot." Wear comfortable, well-padded shorts. You might also benefit from a gel-type saddle.

During the ride, use efficient pacing. Ideally, a double should not consist of one 5-hour and one 7-hour century, but two 6-hour centuries. Don't ride in a paceline that is beyond your ability, and pay attention to your current and average speeds. Use rest stops to clean up, stretch, and eat, but don't overeat. After finishing the double, have a good meal, drink plenty of fluids, and stretch to reduce soreness.

Remember, if the double century becomes too easy, there's always the triple, quadruple, Paris-Brest-Paris, RAAM. . . .

Part Three

TRAINING CONCEPTS

10 FINDING A CADENCE FOR EFFICIENT PEDALING

You hear cycling coaches say it all the time: "Keep your cadence up. Learn how to spin." You're wasting time, they say, unless you're turning the crank about 90 revolutions per minute (rpm). Pedal at this magic number and you're riding like a pro.

Simply put, cadence is a measure of leg speed. Occasional cyclists tend to ride in a relatively high gear at 50 to 60 rpm, which feels natural and comfortable to them. But those who train for fitness and racing must learn to pedal almost twice as fast, between 80 and 110 rpm in moderate gears. Maintaining such a cadence is called spinning.

The Key to Top Performance

It's easy to monitor your cadence while riding. Just count the number of times your right or left foot comes to the top of its pedal stroke in 30 seconds, then multiply by two. The result is your pedal rpm. Some cyclecomputers have a cadence sensor, which does the counting for you. In time, you'll be able to accurately gauge your cadence without checking.

Keep in mind that high cadence is best for top performance. There are several reasons. First, fast riding requires an extremely high rate of work, and you're simply more efficient at a high cadence.

Second, and perhaps most important to racers, a high cadence facilitates rapid acceleration. The reason lies in the mechanics of pedaling. At low cadences in high gears, when a relatively great amount of force is required to turn the pedals, an increase in speed requires a substantial increase in effort. But at high cadences in moderate gears, when there's not as much force being applied, it takes less time and effort to accelerate. Think of it as driving a car with manual transmission. If you want to increase your car's speed quicker, you start in a low gear, before shifting to third or fourth. In the low gear, the higher engine rpm lets you increase a given speed quicker than if you shifted right into fourth.

Third, a fast cadence in a moderate gear requires less effort for each pedal stroke. The faster you spin, the less force is required to rotate the pedals. Thus, you can ride farther with less leg muscle fatigue.

Finally, a fast cadence is easier on the knees. We've all heard of cyclists who have suffered some debilitating trauma from "pushing too big a gear." Doing so results in a relatively slow, struggling pedal stroke that increases the chance of injury.

Finding
the Perfect Cadence

Your perfect cadence depends on your type of riding. For instance, millions of people who use their bicycles for daily transportation pedal merrily along at 40 to 50 rpm. Studies have proven this to be the most efficient cadence for the speeds they normally travel (about 10 mph).

However, for reasons just discussed, road racers favor a pedal rate of 90-plus rpm. In fact, some criterium specialists cruise at 100 rpm or more because of the quick changes in speed their event demands. Conversely, some big-gear time trialists can sustain a powerful stroke best when in the 80 to 85 rpm range. Fast recreational or fitness riders generally perform optimally in gears that let them maintain 90 rpm.

Interestingly, the benefits of spinning begin to disappear above 100 rpm. While the reason is not fully understood, it's probable that such swift leg movement requires more energy than it produces.

Learning to Pedal Faster

It's simple: Shift the chain to an easy gear and leave it there on flat terrain. Concentrate on spinning the pedals smoothly. If you find yourself bouncing on the saddle, reduce the weight on each foot as it travels upward. This should eliminate the rough spots in your pedal stroke and improve comfort. Choose gears that also allow you to spin when climbing and descending. This will further attune your legs to fast pedaling.

In the off-season, practice spinning on rollers or a resistance trainer. Such a workout—without the disruptions of traffic and hills—is perhaps the best way to perfect your spinning technique and become a smooth pedaler. Then, when spring arrives, you can move outdoors and into the world of performance cycling.

11 THE REVEALING STORY BEHIND YOUR VO$_2$ MAX

You're weaving and wheezing up a steep climb, unsure whether you're going to make it. Suddenly, another rider zips by. In a moment, he's crested the hill and disappeared into a glorious descent. Is he taking some performance-enhancing drug? No. Is he packing an engine in his seatbag? Doubtful. He probably just has a higher VO$_2$ max than you.

A Measure of Aerobic Power

VO_2 max is the term used to describe your maximum level of aerobic power. The symbol VO_2 stands for the volume (V) of oxygen (O_2) used per minute. The maximum amount of oxygen that you're able to extract from the air you breathe in during exercise (when you really need it) is your VO_2 max.

This oxygen is transported by the blood to your body tissues. During exercise, more than 90 percent of the oxygen carried by your blood is used by the working muscles. There it meets with carbohydrate and fat molecules derived from the food you've eaten. The oxygen transforms these molecules into usable power, or energy. In essence, VO_2 max is a measurement of how well you turn the air you breathe into energy. Simply, it's the measurement of your aerobic fitness. The higher your VO_2 max, the greater your potential in aerobic endurance sports such as cycling.

The most accurate way to measure your VO_2 max is through a sophisticated test in a human performance laboratory. The test is a demanding one because it involves riding a stationary bicycle until exhaustion. While doing so, you wear a mask or mouthpiece that's connected to a machine via tubes. The machine collects your expired air, analyzes it for oxygen content, and determines your VO_2 max. Such a test usually costs about $100.

What Are Normal VO_2 Max Values?

On the average, a highly trained pro cyclist usually has a VO_2 max of 65 to 75 milliliters/kilogram/minute. This means that during every minute of intense riding, he can deliver 65 to 75 milliliters of oxygen per kilogram of body weight (ml/kg/min) to his working muscles. Looked at another way, a 180-pound (82-kilogram) cyclist with a VO_2 max of 65 uses 5,330 milliliters of oxygen (that's 82 kilograms multiplied by 65 milliliters) in a 60-second maximal aerobic effort—an amazing figure considering the same person needs just 287 milliliters per minute when resting. VO_2 max values for extremely fit females usually measure between 50 and 60, while typical couch potato levels range from 35 to 45.

Are You Born
with a Fixed VO_2 Max?

Nobody knows whether great cyclists are genetically endowed with a high aerobic capacity or whether they build it through training. However, for most of us—who operate well below our ultimate physiological potential—VO_2 max can be improved through training. For instance, it's been repeatedly demonstrated that untrained beginning cyclists can increase their VO_2 max 15 to 20 percent in just 12 to 16 weeks of regular riding.

Once you reach a high level of fitness, however, improvement becomes more difficult. Even if you train consistently all season, you might only improve your VO_2 max by 4 or 5 percent. Conversely, staying completely inactive for three weeks might cost you 27 to 30 percent of your aerobic capacity. Fortunately, you can regain most of your VO_2 max in just ten days of regular training, and all of it in 30 days.

How Can You Improve
Your VO_2 Max?

Intensity is the key to enhancing aerobic capacity. To increase your VO_2 max, emphasize the quality of your training rather than the quantity. Set aside one or two days each week to devote to high-intensity conditioning. Most commonly, this involves doing a series of intervals. Go all-out for 60 or 90 seconds, recover for a minute or two, then do it again. Repeat this 5, 10, or 15 times. Such efforts will increase your VO_2 max.

What's the Bottom Line?

By raising your VO_2 max, you'll become a better cyclist. Unfortunately, raising it by 5 percent doesn't mean you'll see a 5 percent improvement in your riding time. Instead, it might be more like 1 or 2 percent. This is because the faster you ride, the more energy you need to increase speed. For instance, going from 20 to 25 mph is about 30 percent harder than going from 15 to

20 mph. Climbing, which takes place at slower speeds and depends greatly on aerobic conditioning, correlates more directly.

But even a 1 percent annual improvement becomes significant over time. And remember that VO_2 max is just one aspect of cycling performance. As you're increasing your aerobic capacity, you're also building muscle strength and enhancing your riding technique. Alone, each may offer only slight improvements. But together, they spell the difference between being a strong cyclist and weaving and wheezing up those hills.

12 TARGET HEART RATE: THE POINT AT WHICH FITNESS BEGINS

You ride four times a week for a total of 7 hours. A friend cycles six times a week and logs 10 hours. Who is improving their fitness more?

The answer is not as simple as it seems. In fact, the question lacks some crucial information—namely, riding intensity.

The three most important variables in training are: (1) frequency, (2) duration, and (3) intensity. The first two are easily monitored, but the third can be elusive. To determine it, you must know the amount of power you're generating compared to the maximum level you could produce if you were working as hard as possible.

Fortunately, you have a built-in intensity monitor that naturally reports this information. It's your heart rate. It ranges from some minimum value when you're resting to a maximum level during extreme efforts. When riding, your heart rate is at a certain percentage of its maximum. This percentage accurately reflects your exercise intensity. For instance, if your heart rate is at 80 percent of maximum, you're riding at 80 percent intensity.

In the 1950s, researchers discovered that to significantly increase fitness you must maintain an intensity level of at least 65 percent. This value became known as target heart rate. Four decades later, the concept remains the same and is adhered to by most pro cyclists. To increase fitness, their training is geared to hit this physiological bull's-eye.

Determining
Your Target Heart Rate

First you need to find your maximum heart rate. The most accurate way is by taking a laboratory stress test. However, this is expensive and not essential for recreational cyclists.

An alternative is to estimate your maximum heart rate by subtracting your age from 220. Then, multiply the result by 0.65 and 0.85 to determine your target heart rate zone. For instance, if you're 30 years old, your age-predicted max heart rate is 190 beats per minute (220 minus 30). Your target range is 124 (190 times 0.65) to 162 (190 times 0.85) beats per minute (bpm). Whenever you're in this zone—no matter what the exercise—you're training intensely enough to improve cardiovascular fitness. The closer you are to the top of this range, the more benefits you derive.

The Best Way
to Monitor Your Heart Rate

During a ride, there are several ways to check your heart rate. You can monitor your pulse at the carotid artery in your neck (just beside the Adam's apple), or you can check the radial artery in your wrist (at the base of either thumb).

Using your index and middle fingers, count the number of beats in 6 seconds and simply add a zero. Or, to be more accurate, count the number of beats in 15 seconds and multiply by four. It'll take practice before you're able to monitor your pulse quickly and easily while riding. Always make sure the road is clear, and don't slow down because your heart rate will, too.

To simplify things, various electronic pulse monitors are available. These devices typically include a transmitter that straps to the chest and a receiver that fastens around the wrist like a watch. A tiny electrode communicates wirelessly with the receiver, and heart rate readings are displayed.

Good pulse monitors, priced from $125, are accurate and allow heart rate to be tracked throughout a ride. Some models can even interface with computers and generate heart rate graphs.

Using Heart Rate to Attack the Fat

There's a common belief that you will burn more fat calories with low-intensity training. The truth is, at lower intensities, fat does provide a high percentage of fuel. But overall, you can burn more total fat calories by riding harder.

For example, cycling for 1 hour at a heart rate of 120 bpm may burn 350 calories. Of these, about half (175) might be fat calories. Conversely, if you pedal harder and get your heart rate to 160 bpm, you might burn 1,000 calories in an hour. At this intensity, only about a fifth (200) will be fat calories, but that's still 25 more calories than the low-intensity ride. So overall, at the higher intensity, you burn slightly more fat calories and nearly three times as many total calories.

This is doubly significant because of the way our bodies restock used calories. When you ride below your target zone and burn a high percentage of fat calories, your body will replenish these first. Thus, you're back where you started. For losing weight, it's best to ride at the highest level that's comfortably sustainable. Don't restrict your riding intensity in an attempt to burn more fat.

Establishing Your Training Intensity

Evidence generally indicates that the more intensely you train, the more you'll improve. However, it's unknown whether you can reach a point of diminishing returns. Some experts have suggested that 90 percent should be the limit for training intensity. But this has yet to be shown scientifically. Most experts agree that a target range between 65 percent and 85 percent of your maximum rate is safe and effective. If you routinely ride in this target zone, it's guaranteed you'll become more fit.

13 WHAT'S AT THE ANAEROBIC THRESHOLD?

You're flying down the road with a group of riders. The pace is hard but tolerable. Your heart rate is high, but well below maximum. Suddenly, a strong rider moves to the front and the pace quickens. You have a choice. You can drop off the back or increase your effort and stay with the pack. You go for it.

At first you can handle the extra effort. But soon your breathing rate increases dramatically—almost to the point of panting. Then your legs start feeling heavy and even your arms begin to ache. You must slow down.

What happened? Were you in the wrong gear? Did you misjudge your level of fitness? Or were you just having an off day? The answer, most probably, is none of the above. You simply crossed your anaerobic threshold.

A.T., as it's commonly called, is your body's breaking point during exercise. Before reaching it, most of your energy is produced aerobically (with oxygen). But after exceeding it, a significant amount of your energy is produced anaerobically (without oxygen). Anaerobic exercise produces a substance known as lactic acid. It accumulates in the blood and working muscles and disrupts their balance. You feel this happening through such symptoms as breathlessness and muscle burn.

Unfortunately, the mechanisms governing A.T. are not fully understood. In fact, there's disagreement among experts regarding its very definition. However, most agree that once you exceed your A.T., it's impossible to continue at such an intense level for long.

But by exercising at a level just below your A.T., you'll be able to sustain a fast pace longer. This is the guiding principle behind much of the training the pros do. In one study, a group of cyclists was able to ride intensely for 50 minutes staying slightly below their respective A.T.'s. However, not one was able to continue for more than 20 minutes after exceeding the threshold.

Measuring Your A.T.

The most reliable way to assess your A.T. is at a human performance laboratory equipped for testing VO_2 max. Such labs will find your breaking point either by analyzing your ventilatory levels or by drawing blood while you exercise and checking for lactic acid concentration. But it's also possible to estimate your A.T. at home—although such methods rely on the less accurate, even controversial correlation between heart rate and A.T.

One formula is similar to finding your maximum heart rate. It involves subtracting your age from 220, then multiplying that number by 0.85. The result, beats per minute (bpm), is an estimation of your A.T.

Another, more exact method is called Test Conconi (named after the Italian doctor who helped Francesco Moser set several world hour records). To do it, you need a speedometer, a heart rate monitor, a stopwatch, and someone to help you with the recording. Mark a circular course on a flat parking lot or attach your bike to an indoor trainer. After warming up, select a fairly large gear that you won't spin out by the end of the test, and ride for 1 minute at 10 mph. Record your heart rate. Continue to increase your speed 1 mph each minute until you reach exhaustion. Be sure to take careful notes. Record the corresponding heart rates at each 60-second interval. Then make a graph. The horizontal axis is speed cubed (mph × mph × mph). The vertical axis is heartbeats per minute. Plot each point from your test and connect the dots. The resulting line should incline steadily, then bend sharply toward horizontal. According to Conconi, that point is your A.T.

Your A.T. and Your VO₂ Max

Are your anaerobic threshold and your VO_2 max the same? No. As explained in chapter 11, VO_2 max represents your aerobic power, or the maximum amount of oxygen you can extract from the air while exercising. Interestingly, you reach your A.T. long before you reach your VO_2 max. Thus, A.T. is often measured as a percentage of VO_2 max. For instance, if lactic acid starts to accumulate and you begin producing a significant amount of energy without oxygen at 50 percent of your VO_2 max, then this is your A.T.

Which Is More Important?

Your A.T. represents the maximum level of riding intensity that you can sustain. While VO_2 max is important, most people only reach it during the last few moments of intense exercise and can't sustain it. Thus, you rarely operate for long at your VO_2 max. For this reason, many physiologists consider A.T. to be a more important factor in determining cycling performance. The higher your A.T., the harder you can ride for extended periods. Any improvement in your A.T. means a significant upgrading of performance—and a better chance of staying with the pack.

What Are Normal A.T. Values?

For untrained people, typical values are 40 to 70 percent of VO_2 max, with the average being 55 percent. As a cyclist, your threshold will be higher. Some pros have been found to have A.T.'s as high as 85 percent of VO_2 max.

Can You Improve Your A.T.?

Yes. Just as specific training can improve your VO_2 max, it can also raise your A.T. Recent studies demonstrate that long, intense rides, as well as interval training, can raise your threshold. For instance, one study found that training rides done at 80 percent of VO_2 max can improve a beginner's A.T. as much as 70 percent in just nine weeks. Another study showed dramatic A.T. improvements from doing ten 2-minute intervals three days a week at 105 percent of VO_2 max. As you can see, intense riding is the key to increasing A.T.

14 OVERTRAINING: THE DISEASE OF EXCELLENCE

It's a cyclist's worst fear, a coach's nightmare. It's one of the greatest contradictions in sport. The very work, the training, the motivation that produces results leads not to ultimate fitness but to absolute illness. A well-trained cyclist is strong and powerful, but one who has trained too much is weak and powerless. It happens to enthusiastic newcomers and pro racers alike.

William P. Morgan, a pioneer in the field of sports psychology at the University of Wisconsin, calls overtraining the disease of excellence. He explains that training is a double-edged sword in that cyclists must work hard to excel but not so hard that they're overly stressed.

Performance depends on your body's ability to adapt to training. If it's adjusting well, you'll enjoy greater aerobic power, muscle strength, and endurance. But if the training is too intense, your body won't be able to cope and it will eventually break down.

Tell-Tale Signs

The signs of overtraining include insomnia, irritability, elevated waking pulse, higher-than-normal blood pressure, loss of appetite, a sudden drop in weight, and fatigue. If this sounds like a chain reaction, it is. When you can't sleep properly, you become irritable. When you lose your appetite, you lose weight. As your blood pressure and pulse rate rise, so does your basal metabolic rate (the energy cost of living), and fatigue ensues.

Overtraining can also manifest itself psychologically through such symptoms as stress, depression, and staleness. The last is often used as a synonym for overtraining, but according to Morgan, it is more of a result. He explains that in cycling, intense training is necessary for better performance. But when a highly motivated cyclist loses his or her desire to train regularly, he or she may experience staleness. Why? Overtraining.

Contrary to popular belief, overtraining does not result from simply riding too many miles, nor is it confined to elite athletes. Stress plays a crucial role in your body's ability to cope with various training loads. For instance, job stress can have a negative impact on your riding, as can a troubled relationship or a death in the family. In such situations, even a 50-mile-a-week training program might be too much to handle, and overtraining may result. Because it's a constant struggle for many recreational riders to fit cycling into their daily lives, they're often more prone to overtraining than the pros.

How to Avoid Doing Too Much

One of the best ways to recognize overtraining is by keeping a training log or diary. Not only will you have a record of the type of riding you did on any given day, but by keeping track of such things as pulse and weight every morning, you'll also be able to detect overtraining in its early stages—an important advantage, considering some coaches and researchers say it takes six weeks to regain lost performance levels.

You should also rate how you feel in the morning and before you ride, giving yourself an "A" if you feel invincible and an "F" if you can barely get out of bed. Also rate each workout on a scale of 1 (very light) to 10 (extremely difficult). This will help you detect patterns and teach you to listen to your body.

It's also beneficial to periodically have another person assess your performance. This might be a training partner, a spouse, or a coach. Often, they'll uncover nuances you are unaware of.

A New Factor That Can Keep You Riding

A recent development in the study of overtraining might make it easier to detect and combat. It involves the hormones testosterone and cortisol. Research by James Stray-Gunderson at the University of Texas Health Sciences Center found that the level of testosterone in the blood decreases significantly with overtraining in men and women. Meanwhile, the level of cortisol, a stress-response hormone, increases. Thus, when an athlete is overtrained, his or her testosterone/cortisol (T/C) ratio will be lower.

The T/C ratio has proven especially valuable in keeping highly motivated athletes from overtraining. One example is professional triathlete Scott Molina. Despite dwindling success, he needed concrete evidence before he would admit to being severely overtrained. He had a blood test done and the subsequent T/C ratio gave him the incentive he needed to rest, recover, and start winning again.

Beware of Addiction

There's no question that cycling has many tangible physical benefits, including a more efficient and healthy body. But less obvious are its psychological benefits. These include a reduction of anxiety and tension, enhanced self-image and self-confidence, and a general feeling of well-being.

But what happens when this "feel-good" phenomenon becomes addictive? What happens when you can't function unless you have a daily cycling fix?

Connie Chan, a sports psychologist with the University of Massachusetts, treats many "addicted" athletes. Chan explains that "if someone is unable to function in their customary way on a near daily basis without exercise, and if that exercise is not an enhancement but a necessity, the person is likely to be addicted." Chan adds that after two or three days without exercise, susceptible individuals feel less satisfied with themselves, and after five to seven days they may become clinically depressed.

Are You Susceptible?

But who is susceptible? According to Chan, highly disciplined, competitive, Type-A personalities. Surprisingly, the recreational athlete is more likely to become addicted than the pro who views the sport as a livelihood. In either case, the addiction is only realized when the exercise is interrupted.

Some researchers, however, argue that addiction is not the best description of this phenomenon. They say the word has negative connotations. But in his book *Positive Addiction,* author William Glasser discusses how athletes gain strength from their addiction and transfer it to other areas of their lives. Some of these benefits include increases in energy, alertness, confidence, self-awareness, and physical well-being. Among those he studied, the negative aspects of addiction primarily included feelings of guilt about missing exercise sessions.

The Root of the Addiction

Interestingly, at one time it was believed that exercise might be addictive in the classic sense. Opiate-like substances called endorphins are released into the blood during strenuous exercise, and it was theorized that these were the cause of "runner's high" and addictive responses to training. But this has never been proven.

So what then can exercise dependency or addiction be attributed to? Possibly the escape or distraction that exercise provides. For example, Chan substitutes relaxation and meditation therapy for exercise among the athletes she treats. And Glasser found striking similarities among individuals who were positively addicted to running and meditation.

Andrew Jacobs, a sports psychologist who worked with the 1984 U.S. Olympic cycling team, points out that just because you want to ride every day doesn't necessarily mean you're addicted. Generally, there's a problem only when you begin compromising your family life and your job for the sake of training.

Take Action, Take a Break

If you suspect you might be becoming overly dependent on cycling, take a break and reassess your priorities. Think about why you ride. Ask your family and friends for their opinion. Then rearrange your goals accordingly. Occasionally, instead of cycling, sit quietly and think of good rides or races and give your body a chance to catch up with your training. Chances are, some much needed rest will create a sounder mind and body.

Part Four
NUTRITION

15 A NO-NONSENSE GUIDE TO CYCLING NUTRITION

Confused about nutrition? With all the conflicting advice going around, probably the only people who aren't mixed up are the ones who haven't been paying attention. After all, you're regularly bombarded with claims that some food or diet will help you live longer, lose weight, look younger, even ride like a pro.

If you're tired of bouncing from one food fad to another and learning the hard way that radical eating plans, magic ingredients, and expensive supplements don't work, this chapter is for you. It contains all you need to know about eating for good health and optimum performance. Just the facts. No hype. No half-truths. No empty promises.

Carbohydrate, the Best Cycling Fuel

If you had a plate of pasta for every word you've ever read about carbohydrate, you could probably start your own Italian restaurant. There's a reason, however, why sports nutritionists hype carbo: It's your best fuel.

Essentially, carbohydrate is sugar. Simple carbohydrate is a single or double sugar molecule—usually glucose, fructose, galactose, sucrose, or lactose. These are found in nutritional foods (fruits, for instance) as well as less healthful fare, such as candy. Complex carbohydrate is a long chain of simple sugars. It's often called a starch (potatoes and pasta, for example).

When you eat carbo, it's broken down and converted to blood glucose, the body's main fuel and the only type that can feed the brain. Glucose that's not immediately used for energy is stored in the muscles and liver as glycogen to be used later for fuel. If these storage spots are full, the glucose is converted to fat.

Carbohydrate is a better cycling fuel than protein or fat. Although stored protein can be converted to energy when glycogen and glucose become severely depleted, the process is inefficient. Stored fat can also be a fuel source, but it can't be converted to energy in the absence of glucose.

This is why you need carbohydrate. Not only does a high-fat/high-protein diet carry more calories and adverse health effects, it does a poor job of providing energy for your ride.

Getting Enough of the Right Stuff

During and immediately after a hard effort, simple and complex carbo are equally effective. But in your general diet, it's best to emphasize the complex type, which promotes significantly greater glycogen synthesis and offers vitamins, minerals, and fiber along with the energy. Overall, nutritionists recommend that at least 65 percent of your calories come from carbohydrate.

Figuring Your Intake

Unfortunately, most food packages list carbohydrate in grams rather than percentage of calories. This makes determining your intake difficult. To help, follow these two steps.

1. First, determine your total caloric requirement by multiplying your weight by 15.
2. Now add 10 calories (for men) or 8 calories (for women) for each minute of cycling you do a day.

The total is roughly the number of daily calories you need to maintain your weight. (To lose weight, subtract 500 calories per day. You'll lose 1 pound a week.)

For example, a 150-pound man who does a 1-hour training ride would figure as follows: $150 \times 15 = 2,250$ calories + 600 calories (60 minutes $\times$ 10 calories) = 2,850 total calories.

For this rider, 65 percent of total calories would amount to about 1,850. This is the number of carbo calories he should eat daily. Since carbo has 4 calories per gram, he can divide 1,850 by 4 and determine that he needs about 460 grams of carbo a day. (2,850 total calories $\times$ 0.65 = 1,852.5 carbo calories divided by 4 = 463 grams of carbohydrate.)

Beyond the math, the point is that you should dramatically increase your intake of whole-grain breads, nonfat dairy products, cereals, crackers, pasta, rice, potatoes, vegetables, fruits, and juices. At the same time, decrease your intake of fat and protein foods, such as meat, cheese, whole dairy products (use nonfat varieties), and snack items.

Eating to Expand Your Endurance

No matter how well-trained you are, your endurance is limited by one thing: the depletion of your stored glycogen. When this happens, you become light-headed, dizzy, and fatigued. You experience "the bonk." (See chapter 16 for more details on this condition.) Fortunately, though, it is avoidable. There are ways to increase your glycogen stores and prolong performance.

The best way is through training. Well-conditioned muscles can store 20 to 50 percent more glycogen than untrained ones. To take advantage of this expanded capacity, you need to eat plenty of carbohydrate calories every day. Successive days of low intake can lead to a condition called training glycogen depletion, characterized by fatigue and lackluster performance.

In the days before an event, pack your muscles with glycogen by reducing your riding and increasing your intake of carbohydrate to as much as 75 percent of total calories. By putting more glycogen into the muscles—and using less—you'll top off your tank for the big ride. If you have trouble consuming enough food to get all the carbohydrate you need, try a concentrated sports drink, which can supply as much as 235 grams of carbohydrate per 20-ounce serving.

Drink to This

Even Greg LeMond would run out of gas if he didn't refuel while cycling. The reason is simple. Early in a ride, almost all your energy comes from stored muscle glycogen. But as glycogen levels decline, you rely more on blood glucose for fuel. To continue riding, you need to keep these sugar levels high.

One way to do this is with an energy drink. However, if a drink contains too much carbohydrate, it bogs down in the stomach and takes too long to reach the bloodstream, resulting in dehydration and nausea. But the most effective sports drinks contain just enough carbohydrate (5 to 7 percent) to empty into the bloodstream quickly, extending performance without interfering with hydration.

Some cyclists drink juices (often diluted with water) or use sports drinks with high (10 to 25 percent) carbohydrate concentrations without problems. When mixing an energy drink or diluting a fruit juice, experiment with different concentrations.

To be effective, a sports drink should deliver about 40 to 60 grams of carbohydrate per hour. With most brands, you can accomplish this by drinking 1½ to 2 standard water bottles an hour.

For best results, avoid products with fructose (which is absorbed slowly). Look instead for sucrose, glucose, or glucose polymers. The last consists of several glucose molecules linked together. This chain is absorbed quickly, as if it were a single molecule. But in the bloodstream it breaks up, and you get the benefit of several glucose molecules instead of just one.

If you prefer solid food on the bike, try energy bars or other high-carbohydrate selections such as bagels, bananas, or dried fruit. Unlike drinks, these choices do not enhance hydration. So drink plenty of water with them.

A Matter of Fat

Next to carbohydrate, fat is your body's best fuel. It's primarily useful on long, slow rides, when your intensity is low. But don't assume this gives you license to eat all the ice cream and french fries you want. We all have plenty of stored fat and, in fact, most of us have too much. While we can store only limited amounts of glycogen, we can stockpile unlimited fat, which can be burned only in the presence of glucose. For this reason, what we need is carbohydrate, not more fat.

This isn't to say body fat is useless. It does store vitamins and provide insulation. But in excess, it's one of the biggest health risks imaginable. It increases susceptibility to heart disease, high blood pressure, certain cancers, and diabetes.

Any kind of food can turn into body fat if you eat too much. But not surprisingly, the most likely source for body fat is dietary fat. Compared to protein and carbohydrate, dietary fat has more than twice the calories (9 instead of 4 per gram) and appears to be stored more readily.

For optimal health and performance, nutritionists recommend that you derive no more than 30 percent of your total calories from fat, and no more than 10 percent from the saturated fats found primarily in animal products. The remainder should be the unsaturated form that comes from vegetable oils, nuts, and grains.

How to Trim Your Diet

One way to assure a low fat intake is to check nutrition labels and select foods with less than 3 grams of fat per 100 calories. To be more specific and discover exactly what percentage of a particular food is fat, use this calculation: Check the product's nutrition label and multiply the grams of fat by 9. Then divide that number by the total calories in the food. The result is percentage of calories from fat. For example, 1 ounce of Velveeta Process Cheese Spread has 80 calories and 6 grams of fat. The calculation is: 6 grams of fat × 9 calories per gram of fat = 54 fat calories. Fifty-four divided by 80 total calories = 67.5 percent of calories from fat. (To figure a food's percentage of calories from carbohydrate or protein, multiply the number of grams of that nutrient by 4 instead of 9, then divide by total calories.)

You can trim fat from your diet by reducing your intake of animal foods. When you do consume them, select lean cuts of meat, skinless poultry, and nonfat dairy products. Also, cut down on butter and margarine, salad dressings, and hydrogenated and tropical oils, which are prevalent in many baked goods.

Interestingly, the fitter you are, the quicker you'll burn fat. A well-trained body is capable of bringing more oxygen into the muscles, thus increasing the rate of fat metabolism and sparing some glycogen stores.

Protein: Enough Already

Cyclists use more protein than sedentary people. But this doesn't mean you have to increase your protein intake. In fact, you're probably already getting more than you need.

One reason cyclists need extra protein is for fuel. Once muscles have depleted their primary source (carbohydrate), they begin using protein, according to new studies.

"Protein can be a small but significant source of energy—about 5 to 10 percent of total energy needs," says Michael J. Zackin, Ph.D., of the University of Massachusetts Medical School. "Protein calories become increasingly important in carbohydrate-depleted states. If you train more than an hour a day and begin to deplete glycogen stores, you become increasingly dependent on body protein for energy."

The Recommended
Daily Allowance

Although results vary widely, Dr. Zackin says cycling may raise your protein requirements 20 to 90 percent beyond U.S. Recommended Daily Allowances. The USRDA is 0.363 grams of protein per pound of body weight. For a 150-pound man, this is about 54 grams a day; for a 120-pound woman, about 43 grams. Consider the 20 to 90 percent, and the male cyclist's daily protein intake rises to 65 to 103 grams, the woman's to 52 to 82 grams.

Interestingly, most active people are already at these levels or beyond. This was illustrated in a study of eight highly trained women cyclists. Although their diets fell short of recommended values for many nutrients, their protein intake was 145 percent of the recommended amount.

High protein levels aren't hard to reach. For instance, 3 ounces of meat, fish, or poultry contains 21 grams. A cup of beans has 14 grams, 3 tablespoons of peanut butter has 12, and a cup of nonfat milk contains 9. All this adds up quickly. In fact, the average American consumes 100 grams a day.

The Best Sources

So unless you're a strict vegetarian or chronic dieter, don't worry about increasing your protein intake. Instead, worry about where your protein comes from. The best sources are low in fat and include a healthy dose of complex carbohydrate. Muscles are built by work, not extra protein, and work is best fueled by carbohydrate.

Some low-fat, high-protein choices include whole grains, beans, vegetables, fish, skinless poultry, soy products, lean cuts of meat, and nonfat dairy products. Even vegetarians can get plenty of high-quality protein with a varied diet combining grains, legumes, nuts, seeds, vegetables, dairy products, and eggs.

Overall, nutritionists say 15 percent of your diet should be protein calories. But don't sweat it. This is one nutrition goal you'll reach without even trying.

16 HOW TO EAT TO BEAT "THE BONK"

You've been riding for several hours, feeling great and enjoying the scenery. But for the last 15 minutes your riding partner has been talking continuously and it's beginning to irritate you. Halfway up the next hill, you reach for the shift lever and discover that you're already in your lowest gear. You struggle toward the top, where your partner is waiting with a curious look on his face.

"What's the jerk smiling about?" you wonder. "This is a stupid ride, anyway. I should have stayed home and mowed the lawn."

Wait a minute. What's going on here? A few minutes ago you felt great, now you feel terrible. Why?

Simply put, you've bonked. This term is traditional in cycling. You'll hear it over and over again. It describes the symptoms that occur when you deplete essential carbohydrate stores in your body as a result of sustained exercise. To scientists, the resulting condition is called hypoglycemia.

What's Happening to Your Energy

As you ride, most of the fuel being oxidized or burned is consumed by your active muscles. Both fat and carbohydrate can be utilized for this process. Fat, stored in fatty tissue, is reduced to free fatty acids and is transported by the blood to the working muscles. In contrast, carbohydrate is stored within the muscles as glycogen, which is a long polymer composed of many glucose molecules. During exercise, individual molecules are removed from the polymer and used as energy.

However, your vital organs also require a continuous supply of fuel. Whether at rest or during exercise, your brain and nervous system, for instance, depend upon blood glucose. The reason for this dependence is that the cells of your nervous system don't store glycogen and can't use fat. Thus, to meet energy requirements, blood glucose levels must be tightly regulated and maintained. This job is largely done by the liver, which contains large stores of glycogen that can be converted to glucose.

With the muscles and organs vying for glucose, extended exertion can drain the liver. When blood glucose levels become too low to meet the fuel requirements of your central nervous system, you begin feeling disoriented, tired, irritated, and generally miserable. In a word, you bonk.

A Quick Solution

Fortunately, you can remedy the bonk. When your blood glucose levels fall as a result of liver glycogen depletion, you can replenish them by simply eating or drinking something rich in carbohydrate. This is quickly digested into simple sugars that enter the bloodstream and are transported to the liver, muscles, and other organs.

Even better, you can avoid the bonk altogether by periodically eating or drinking small amounts of carbohydrate while riding. This allows your stomach to continuously add glucose to the blood, thereby greatly reducing the drain on your liver's valuable glycogen stores. The trick is to begin eating or drinking about 15 minutes into a long ride and continue to do so every 10 to 15 minutes thereafter. Even on relatively short rides, never leave home without your favorite energy food and/or drink—just in case.

When Your Muscles Hit the Wall

"Hitting the wall" and "bonking" are terms often used interchangeably, but there is an important difference. Both result from fuel depletion. However, unlike bonking, which is caused by the depletion of liver glycogen, hitting the wall stems from the depletion of muscle glycogen. Bonking is avoidable and curable. Hitting the wall can be delayed by ingesting carbohydrate, but once it happens, you're essentially finished for the day.

As your rate of fuel consumption rises in response to intensifying exercise, your muscles turn to their most readily available fuel—muscle glycogen. In fact, it's the only fuel that can support exercise at levels greater than 70 percent of VO_2 max. (Another reason muscle glycogen is so important is that it provides an essential intermediate product that's required to burn fat.) When you run out of muscle glycogen, you're only able to exercise at very moderate intensity.

The Key to Avoiding Hitting the Wall

As with beating the bonk, the key to avoiding hitting the wall is maintaining a steady intake of carbohydrate. It's also important not to waste the muscle glycogen you have. For instance, each time you accelerate rapidly on the bike, your body switches to anaerobic metabolism to meet the extra energy demands. This process uses glycogen much less efficiently than aerobic metabolism. Therefore, on long rides, always accelerate smoothly, avoid blasting up hills, and don't be tempted into riding harder than usual.

And keep eating and drinking foods high in carbohydrate. Like a pro road racer, chew almost continuously on energy bars, fig cookies, fruit bars, bananas, dried fruit, granola bars, jam sandwiches, etc., and consume at least one bottle of an energy drink each hour.

Experiment with on-bike foods until you find those that are most palatable and effective. Then remember to eat them. It's amazing how even experienced riders bonk or hit the wall with their pockets full of food. On a ride that will exceed 2½ hours, never let 15 minutes go by without sipping or nibbling.

17 WHAT RACERS REALLY EAT FOR POWER

An Italian superstar, leader of a big stage race, hunches over a breakfast table, scarfing plate after plate of food. From nearby, a rival team director studies the champion's mouth as he might another rider's legs.

The Italian is eating too much too fast, he figures. So later, when the coach gathers his charges for a final pre-stage briefing, he tells them the leader hasn't eaten properly and will be vulnerable to attack.

Midway up the day's first climb, his riders move as instructed to the front of the pack and raise the pace. And sure enough, the gluttonous champion is left behind, wishing his water bottles contained bicarbonate of soda instead of H_2O.

This incident happened more than a decade ago, during an era when racers generally paid less attention to what they ate and how they ate it than they do now. Today, nutritional awareness is just one aspect of the comprehensive scientific approach to the sport that most pros take. While no one claims that eating right is the sole route to victory, most say eating poorly can prevent success—just as it did for one ravenous Italian.

A Nutritional Mission

Pro bike racers eat more than other athletes. During a stage race such as the Tour de France, they may burn close to 250,000 calories (9,000 per day) and must continually strive to replace them.

Fluid replacement is equally important, of course. As the nine-man 7-Eleven team struggled through the torrid mountain stages of the 1990 Tour, each racer chugged as many as 15 bottles of liquid per 6-hour leg. But sometimes even this isn't enough. Davis Phinney finished one of the latter stages so dehydrated and weak that he had to receive fluid intravenously throughout the night.

While pro cyclists consume astounding quantities of food and drink, their basic nutritional mission is the same as yours. They try to maximize their intake of complex carbohydrate to ensure a steady supply of energy, and they fight a constant battle against fat that could slow them on hills. Pros steer clear of deep-fried foods. Heavy sauces are left unladled. Mayonnaise rarely leaves the refrigerator. The goal is a daily caloric intake that's close to 65 percent carbohydrate, 20 percent fat, and 15 percent protein. And most racers come close to achieving it.

Feasts Fit
for Kings (of the Road)

Trainers Trudi Roberts and Jodi Wallner are responsible for buying, preparing, and distributing much of the food eaten by the 7-Eleven team in Europe. "It's an incredible amount," says Roberts.

"We have to go to the grocer at least once a day—sometimes twice."

Beginning with Breakfast

During the Tour, breakfast typically begins 3 hours before the stage. The first course includes coffee or tea, cereal, bread (white, wheat, or pumpernickel), a muesli/fruit/yogurt mix, corn flakes or crisp rice cereal, granola, soy milk, jam, honey, and croissants (although some racers avoid this buttery temptation).

"They're always watching what they eat," says Roberts, "particularly when the race enters the mountains." According to team director Jim Ochowicz, "The riders don't want to overfuel in the hills. They want lighter food and try not to carry a lot of bulk in their stomachs."

Just when an observer might think breakfast complete, a second course of heavier, hot dishes is rolled in, including rice, spaghetti, omelettes or boiled eggs, and chicken, fish, or steak. Meat is common in pro racing and is espoused for its protein content, which is instrumental in rebuilding and maintaining muscle tissue. "Our doctor prescribes that the riders should have plenty of protein in the morning," says Ochowicz.

Food to Go

At the race start, more food is spread in the cargo space of the team car for the riders to stuff in their jersey pockets or munch on. Offerings include Champagne (a syrupy French fruit juice), which is poured into 4-ounce bottles and used on particularly hot days when solid food is difficult to ingest; energy bars, cut in half in their wrappers for easy eating; a thick pudding made of semolina, milk, raisins and sugar, cut in squares and wrapped; two or three pieces of fruit; and *pannini,* which are soft-roll sandwiches that include either ham and cheese or rice pudding and jam. (The top is removed and the mixture put inside.)

These same foods are packed in the two "musettes" (feed bags) that the riders receive during a typical Tour stage. Sometimes a fresh bakery tart is included as a special treat. Throughout the day, the riders also receive carbohydrate drink—as many as six bottles, in addition to about the same amount of water.

Pro Meals
for 1-Day Events

For one-day races, riders tend not to eat as much the day of the event because nutritional needs can be satisfied with careful carbohydrate loading. "You can build for a one-day race with nutrients and calories a week in advance," says Ochowicz. "In a stage race, you must provide continual refueling."

The night before the 156-mile CoreStates U.S. Pro Championship in Philadelphia, trainers Julie Haskell and Patty Spillner spent nearly 3 hours assembling musette bags for their Coors Light team. The floor of their hotel room was covered with trays of ripe fruit—apricots, peaches, plums, grapes, bananas, and kiwis. They also made an assortment of pannini.

Early in a long one-day race, riders will eat meat pannini, often a combination of low-fat turkey slices and apple butter. Another popular blend is strawberry jam and cream cheese. In the course of a 6-hour event, a rider will eat two or three.

Other staples are fruit pies, baked cakes (cut long and wrapped in foil), soft cookies, and rice pudding in plastic bags (riders bite off a corner and squeeze it into their mouth).

"Some of this race food is very fatty," admits Coors Light team director Len Pettyjohn. "Our guys eat it because it tastes good, feels good, and is available everywhere. But a few cookies and some pannini account for a relatively small proportion of their total daily intake."

When the racers approach a feed zone, they'll sometimes yell for the drink they want, says Haskell. It's either water, an energy drink, or late in a race, cola for a caffeine boost.

The Post-Race Meal

Immediately after each Tour stage, 7-Eleven riders are given water, juice, fruit, bread, and biscuits to help fortify their depleted bodies. "And if it's been a hard day, we give them something special from the bakery," says Roberts.

According to Ochowicz, a stage race such as the Tour involves "24-hour refueling. The guys are continually concerned with recuperation and food." So after the post-race tailgate, the riders find a meal waiting in their hotel rooms. It includes sandwiches, low-fat yogurt, two pieces of fruit, juice, bottled water, and maybe a quiche or pizza. A few hours later, following showers, massage, and rest, it's time for the real eating to begin—dinner.

Typically, the evening meal starts with pasta. Because of the huge amounts the riders require, different varieties are used, such as spaghetti, risotto, or tortellini. Next comes salad, soup, and a protein source such as meat or fish, followed by a pastry dessert and fruit.

Then, just a few hours later, it all begins again.

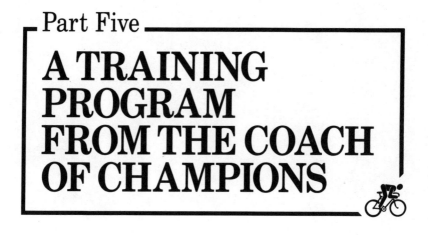

Part Five

A TRAINING PROGRAM FROM THE COACH OF CHAMPIONS

18 MIKE WALDEN'S PROVEN YEAR-ROUND PROGRAM

"Tell me about your grandfather."

So begins a training consultation with the venerable Mike Walden. Although he's been blind in one eye since birth, this coach's stare is piercing, implacable. You have his complete attention; you're all that exists for him. He leans closer, resting two hands on his falcon-head cane. The interrogation continues. He wants to know your family history, what time you rise, how many hours you work, what your father did for a living. Suddenly, he reaches forward, pinches a fold of skin on your upper arm, and pronounces the unhappy verdict: 20 percent body fat.

In short, before Walden prescribes a program for you, he's going to know as much about you as your mother does. He could write your biography.

"I create cyclists in their image," says Walden. "I do not create clones."

A Coach of 300 Medalists

It's an approach that has brought considerable results. By his estimate, Walden, now in his seventies, has trained some 300 of America's world and national championship medalists through his Detroit-based Schwinn Wolverines Sports Club. This includes four-time world champ Connie Young, seven-time world medalist Sue Novara-Reber, Motorola pro Frankie Andreu, and Tour de France stage winner Jeff Pierce.

On the Program

To learn more about what it means to be "on the program," as Walden's protégés fondly refer to his training system, *Bicycling* attended a one-week session of the Walden School of Cycling in Mount Plymouth, Florida.

One thing was quickly apparent: Walden's students speak of their coach with religious fervor. This is because being on his program involves nothing less than a complete lifestyle change— a sort of cyclists' EST. While you needn't surrender your savings, you will do breathing exercises at 7 A.M., twice-daily walks with hand weights, self-massage, and a litany of other things that are good for your body. Life according to Walden even includes a method for chewing food.

Sound hard-core? Don't be put off. Walden emphasizes that what he teaches is simply a healthy lifestyle, equally applicable to pro racers, sport riders, and even sedentary people. Being on his program also involves using a fixed gear, hitting a punching bag, and doing plenty of early-season miles on the small chainring. The last directive is engraved in the minds of all his students. At the Florida camps, you are not allowed to sully your big ring. To do so could result in a threat from the falcon-head cane. The reason? You must learn to pedal fast in full circles before you can pedal hard. Proper pedaling technique is one of the many "disciplines" or building blocks that form the basis of Walden's successful program. Cycling, no less than ballet or basketball, is comprised of specific skills that must be mastered, according to the coach.

The 4 Walden Basics

The following four chapters cover the basic principles of Walden's program, told in his words. The first covers training basics, riding position, pedaling technique, daily routine, and nutrition, in addition to a sample cycling program. The second details his specific disciplines, including group riding, cornering, climbing, and bike handling. The third discusses additional skills

Mike Walden is always with his riders—a "voice" in their helmets, telling them when to shift, attack, or rest.

and special workouts to build speed, power, and endurance. Finally, Walden outlines his winter program, including cross-training and beginning the annual conditioning cycle. In all, it constitutes a proven, season-long system for improving your riding.

19 THE ESSENTIAL ELEMENTS OF BETTER TRAINING

Although I'll give you as much information as possible on improving performance, you should know right off that the most important thing is to have a coach. I like to sit down with new riders and find out what they're like. I want to know their sports background and what kind of program they've been on. There's no sense changing things if the rider is already successful. A good coach knows this.

Determining Goals

The next thing is to determine goals. I ask people to shoot high. Sometimes, when a rider tells me he or she wants to become a Category II racer, I say, "I'm not interested in that. If you decide you want to make the national team, then come back and see me." But it depends on the person. The flip side is that you must make it fun. For example, if you're going to be what I call a super-tourist (fast recreational rider) and not a racer, fine. You can be what you want to be. The number one thing is to enjoy yourself. You need to progress and work at it, but if it isn't fun, you're not going to stay with it.

Learning the Keys to Self-Coaching

It's essential that you keep a log book detailing your workouts, gearing, food, pulse rate, and anything else that's pertinent to your training. I recommend using an "active" rather than a resting pulse to gauge your training. I think it's more consistent. Take it at midday before eating. If it's more than five beats per minute above normal, you may need rest.

While it's important to consult a coach, it's also crucial to learn to coach yourself. This can't be overemphasized. Often, when a rider asks me a question, such as what gear he or she should use in a time trial, my response is: "Don't ask me. Look in your log book." Everyone is different.

3 Major Mistakes Riders Make

Next, I work on correcting the three major mistakes that all new riders make. Believe it or not, the first one is that they don't properly inflate their tires. Obviously, that's simple to remedy. The next two are establishing proper position on the bike and developing an efficient pedal stroke using the proper gears.

Riding Position

Riding position involves compromises. For instance, what's most aerodynamic may not give the highest power output, and vice versa. Generally, it takes two years of experimentation to establish what's best for you.

The beginning rider would do well to visit a shop using the Fit Kit bicycle-sizing system. It gives you a good starting point. But it's for the average person, and that may not be you. That's why I tell people it's a mistake not to get on the Fit Kit when you start, but it's a big mistake to get on it after you've been riding and fine-tuning your position for a while.

In any case, one of the first things I look for is about a 30-degree angle between the rider's upper body and the ground when the hands are on the drops. We use what I call a target board, which is basically a large piece of Masonite with lines drawn at 15, 30, and 45 degrees. I'll take a photo of the rider in front of this board. We'll do this periodically as changes are made. It serves as a reference point.

The other thing I look for is an angle of 12 to 18 degrees behind the knee when the crankarm is down and in line with the seat tube. This is based on observing top riders. It also directly affects pedaling technique, as I'll discuss later. If your saddle is too high, you'll pedal toes-down, which overemphasizes your calf muscles.

Another key factor is weight distribution. Most riders are back-end heavy. That's like putting sandbags in the trunk of a car. You can't steer, brake, or control your vehicle as well. Also, if the bar is too close, you can't pull the bike back underneath you in an emergency. This could cause you to touch a wheel and go down.

For these reasons I recommend a weight distribution of 48 percent in front and 52 percent in back with your hands on the drops. Use a bathroom scale under one wheel and a phone book of equal height under the other. Get on, take a reading, reverse the bike, and do it again. Make changes by altering stem length or bar height.

Smoothing the Pedal Stroke

Pedaling is the essence of our sport. Everyone thinks I'm small-gear crazy, but pedaling fast for long periods helps develop the proper neuromuscular pathways. You must first learn how to pedal quickly, then you can slow it down and develop power. Don't start by teaching yourself to pedal slowly because it's a hard process to reverse.

Here's another way to think of it. During a hard group ride or race, it's comparatively easy to recover if you're winded from pedaling too fast. In fact, it might only take getting over the next hill. But if your legs are spent from pushing a big gear, it can take 48 hours or more to recover.

Building speed with low gears. Some riders think that emphasizing low gears limits their speed. Not so. My club regularly does 30-mph training sprints in a 42 × 16-tooth gear. Of course, these riders use bigger gears in races. But it shows what you can do when you learn the technique. Pedal speeds of more than 160 rpm are possible.

Consequently, I emphasize using a fixed gear in the early season. I'm also a firm believer in track riding and doing one-

legged pedaling for short distances. For instance, start every ride
with 100 yards of right-legged pedaling, then switch to the left
for another 100 yards. These activities force you to pedal in circles. You must learn to apply pressure all the way around the
stroke and stay "ahead" of the pedals.

Avoiding fatigue. It's directly related to fatigue, too. You'll
last longer using small gears. As an analogy, let's say you want to
move a ton of cement across the street, and it's all in 100-pound
bags. One approach is to say, "This is too much walking. I'll take
it 200 pounds at a time." You can only do three or four trips like
that before you're exhausted. But you can move that cement all
day 100 pounds at a time because your circulation is up, and
you're not burning a tremendous amount of energy. You must
keep fresh blood circulating through the muscles.

This is why everything you do on a bike must be relaxed.
You can't have muscles fighting other muscles, and you must
avoid lactic acid buildup. The secret is plenty of miles in a fixed
gear and emphasizing small gears throughout the season. It
teaches your muscles the proper firing sequence. You expend
energy in a certain part of the stroke, and the rest of the time
that muscle is relaxed. One muscle group cuts in and another
cuts out. Instead of it being mechanical, the reflex becomes
automatic.

On the road, this means downshifting before you need to.
Say you round a corner and suddenly you're going into the wind.
Most riders grind out the gear, and pretty soon they can't maintain
it anymore due to lactic acid buildup. Inevitably, their speed
drops. What they should have done is downshifted right away.
This is a climbing technique we use, too. Shift to a lower gear
before you need it.

The foot and shin. I put a lot of emphasis on the angle
formed by the foot and shin. I advocate a neutral pedaling style
in which this angle is 90 degrees most of the time. However,
there is a natural heel-to-toe transition that occurs, just as it does
when walking. You should drag the pedal down with your heel,
pull it back at the bottom of the stroke, and then kick across the
top. By allowing the foot/shin angle to open and shut this way,
the muscles of the upper leg contract, relax, and flush out the
lactic acid.

You'll lose efficiency if you're primarily a toes-down pedaler,
though it's natural to use this technique at extremely fast pedal

speeds, such as during sprints. Conversely, you don't want to overemphasize the heel-down technique, though it can be useful at slower cadences, such as when climbing.

Developing a Daily Routine

Think about performance 52 weeks of the year. This doesn't mean going hard all the time. But it does mean taking care of yourself.

A Morning Ritual

Start each day with a wake-up routine before breakfast. Scrub your entire body with the palms of your hands to force blood to these areas and supply them with oxygen. Next, jitterbug jog in place for 2 minutes to further stimulate circulation. Follow this with a series of static stretches (no bouncing), holding each one for 15 seconds. These include trunk twists, toe touches (cross the legs and reach down), and pulling the arms across the body. Roll your head gently in both directions. Do isometric neck exercises, gently pushing the palms of your hands against the front and sides of the head for 15 seconds at a time. This helps build neck strength that could prevent injury in a crash.

Next, do three sets of 10 of the following exercises to further stimulate blood flow: jumps (sink low with knees bent, explode upward reaching your hands to the sky, land with knees bent), push-ups, and crunches for the abdomen.

Then do 5 deep-breathing exercises. These are essential for eliminating stale air from your lungs and building the cardiovascular system. Even trained athletes use only 40 to 50 percent of lung capacity. Inhale normally, hold it for 2 seconds, then inhale more as hard and fast as possible while raising your hands above your head. After 4 seconds, exhale slowly through pursed lips. Bend at the waist and exhale for 6 more seconds, expelling every last bit of air from your lungs while using your arms to squeeze the chest. The whole thing is predicated on the exhale. It helps develop your breathing muscles and recruits more of the lung's alveoli (air sacs).

Massage after the Ride

Another essential part of the daily routine is massage. After a ride this helps eliminate lactic acid. Lie on your back and prop your legs against the wall, or do it in a warm bath. Rub your legs toward your heart to increase circulation. To loosen the buttocks, sit and roll on a tennis ball.

I'm also a big proponent of short walks as a means to speed recovery following hard rides, prevent soreness, and aid digestion after meals. It's something you can do any place, any time. You can build upper-body strength by combining it with vigorous arm movements using hand weights. This simulates the motion of pulling on the handlebar and helps provide strength for cornering and bumping other riders.

Learning to Eat Properly

People tend to think of every aspect of training except nutrition. However, this area has provided one of the greatest benefits to athletes in this century.

Choosing the Right Foods

In general, the American diet is awful. The food is grown with chemicals. You should buy natural, organic food, if possible. There's a strong case for being a vegetarian, except that it can be hard to find the right foods when you're traveling. And you have to be careful not to miss the things that meat supplies, such as protein.

Don't eat fried foods. Also, avoid "whites"—sugar, flour, and whole milk. I believe raw sugar and molasses are better sweeteners than white sugar, and whole wheat flour is better than white flour. In general, eat the least processed foods. The more refined foods are, the more difficult it is to get energy from them. For example, if you're a meat-eater and you have a choice between a hamburger and a piece of chuck beef, take the chuck beef. The less it's processed, the better.

The Right Way
to Eat a Meal

It's extremely important to chew your food thoroughly. All my athletes are taught this. It's the way to extract the maximum food value. You must mix the food with saliva, which is loaded with enzymes. I even recommend "chewing" energy drinks by moving the jaw around to get those digestive enzymes mixed in.

Also, you should never drink and eat at the same time because this sends false signals to your gut. It also dilutes the gastric juices used in digestion. And don't eat when you are extremely tired because digestion requires energy. Don't eat right before bed, either.

Eating on the Road

What should you consume during a ride or race? Don't ask me. Look in your log book. Experiment with high-carbohydrate foods or what I call high-tech water (energy drinks), and see what works for you. Ask yourself, "What did I eat yesterday, and how did I perform? How much did I eat? Did I bonk?" Conduct constant experiments. Nobody can write a prescription for you.

Concerning on-bike nutrition, however, two things are crucial, and you've heard them before: Eat before you're hungry, and drink before you're thirsty.

A Weekly Program

I have a very specific, incremental approach to the yearly program that includes plenty of cross-training and at least 250 hours of riding using a fixed gear. This will be covered in chapter 22. For now, let's assume you have a base of at least 1,000 miles on the small chainring. What should you be doing each week? Here's a sample program.

Monday: This is the day for a recovery ride. Pedal easily in a small gear for an hour or so.

Tuesday: Sprints. In Detroit, the Wolverine club trains on an island that's about 5½ miles around. Usually we do two intervals down one side and two up the other, in a group. The speed picks up at a designated spot, and we sprint for a predetermined finish. By yourself, you could do five sprints of various lengths: 150 to 500 meters, or 1200 to 1500 meters, with almost full recovery in between. Start by doing these at 75 percent of full effort and increase 5 percent each week.

Wednesday: Steady ride, preferably with a group in a paceline. This should be as far as the event you're training for, but at a much lower intensity. Each rider swings off upon reaching the front. Walk with hand weights in the evening.

Thursday: Road racing simulation or a fast group ride, with 20 percent of the total ride done at top speed. This includes five sprints of various lengths (longer than those on Tuesday).

Friday: Easy ride for recovery.

Saturday: Endurance ride.

Sunday: Long race/fast group ride.

Warm Up, Cool Down

Every ride should begin with a warm-up and end with a cooldown. But warm-up doesn't mean pedaling easily. Increase your gear and effort with jumps, duplicating the effort of a hard ride or race. For instance, accelerate to 20 mph, slow to 18, accelerate to 23, slow to 21, and so on, until you reach fast cruising speed. This will decrease the time it takes to reach your second wind, the physiological state when oxygen distribution catches up with your activity level. Once the warm-up is completed, your cardiovascular system will be able to quickly supply oxygen to the muscles demanding it. For the cool-down, spin easily for 10 minutes in a low gear.

Staying on Track

During endurance rides, it's important to finish what you set out to do. If I tell you to ride 50 miles, but you feel ill and tell me you're only capable of 25, that's fine. But you must complete the entire 25 miles. The first time you quit makes it easier to quit the second time.

Speedwork is a different matter. Do as much of the workout as you can at the desired speed and intensity. If you can't do 80 meters (or whatever distance) at the speed you want to, then shorten it to 60 meters. If you can't do that, then you're through for the day.

A lot of riders go too hard on the "on" days and too hard on the "off" days. They wind up saying, "Well, a little bit of poison is good for me, so a lot ought to be great." This doesn't necessarily work. If you're not rested, you're never going to develop.

20 THE KEY DISCIPLINES OF BIKE HANDLING

I sometimes call my program proficient cycling because I believe the sport is composed of specific skills. Just as baseball players attend spring training to work on throwing and catching, we conduct the Walden School of Cycling in Florida to work on what I call the disciplines: cornering, pacelines, sprinting, climbing, bike handling, and so on.

Practice Makes Perfect

The only way to learn is by repetition. That's why my coaches hack on riders until they get these things right. Do you want to learn how to ride in a paceline? Then you must do it all the time—even if you're just going 100 yards to the next stop sign. If you lay off and don't practice, your timing will be bad. Consequently, in a race you might not close a gap in time, or you might bump wheels and crash. During a century, you might slide out in a fast corner because you didn't practice shifting your weight.

Once you perfect all the skills, you develop what I call an unshakable ego because you've analyzed the situation and know you can do something better than someone else. You can concentrate on playing the game. You don't worry about whether you're going to get through the next turn or not. Instead you're thinking: "How am I going to make it tougher for the other guy to get around the corner?"

It works at any level. If you're a fast recreational rider ("super tourist"), you can use the skills to make cycling easier and safer. If you're a racer, you use them to go faster and—who knows?— maybe someday become good enough to ride professionally. Whatever you learn will serve you well, no matter what you aspire to.

Keep in mind that what I do is teach people how to ride. What I can't do is teach you how to race or perform at your absolute potential. You teach yourself that. This is why your training diary is essential. Chances are you already know your strong points. The key is to ask yourself, "How can I be beaten?" or "What kept me from finishing that century in less than 6 hours?" Work to eliminate shortcomings.

Discipline 1:
Steering through a Corner

Steering is a lost art. Most cyclists turn their bikes by leaning into a corner. When you steer, you use the handlebar and headset deliberately, more akin to driving a car. You also keep the bike more upright. It's the fastest, safest way, but few do it.

Here's another way to think of it. When turning, the bike and rider remain in the same plane. The lean angle is determined by the tightness of the corner, pedal clearance, speed, and road quality. The risk is that you'll lean too far and slide out. But when you steer, you break the plane of bike and rider by shifting your weight to the inside, over the top tube. The bike can slip and move sideways, but you won't crash. I've seen pros do this in wet races on cobblestones. In every corner the bike slips 4 or 5 inches, but the rider stays up. It's not just a racing tactic, it's a safety factor.

Fast Corners

Here's how to do it. Shift your weight slightly forward, twist at the hips, and put your nose directly over the inside brake lever. Pull up on the inside of the handlebar by bending that arm.

Coach Mike Walden's advice for fast, safe cornering is to steer the bike rather than lean it.

Meanwhile, push down on the outside with a nearly straight arm. Keep your knees in and continue pedaling to maintain traction. (See the photo above.)

There are many other advantages to steering. In a corner you can accelerate while others are coasting because their extreme lean angle doesn't allow pedaling. You can also steer through a pack of riders where there isn't enough room to lean.

Pacelines

When riding in a paceline, steer and push your bike in behind the last rider after dropping back, making sure your body is away from that person. Why? Because if you hit that person's rear wheel with your front, you can pull your bike back underneath you and avoid a crash. If you were leaning, you would crash.

Practicing Steering

To practice steering I use the "cul-de-sac drill." Find one that's a perfect circle, about 35 feet in diameter with no traffic or pavement irregularities, or use a parking lot. Enter it by briefly steering to the right, then travel counterclockwise, steering to the left. Circle it ten times. Exaggerate the motion by placing your weight way to the inside (nose over the inside brake lever), pushing down on the outside of the bar with a straight arm, and pulling up on the inside with a bent arm. Don't forget to pedal because a driven bike has more traction than a coasting one. (I teach my riders to pedal almost all the time— even when descending or going to the back of a paceline.) Exit the cul-de-sac by steering to the right, then reverse direction and repeat.

Keep in mind that there is only one correct line to take through a corner. Strive for the shallowest arc possible. Start wide, cut to the apex, then swing wide again. And if you must brake, do so before entering the corner. Otherwise you can lose traction.

Discipline 2:
Bumping and Dodging

No matter what type of riding you do, you should be accustomed to contact from other cyclists. If you know how to do it and practice, there's no reason why a little bumping should cause you to lose control and crash. The riders I coach think nothing of pedaling down the road leaning and bumping against each other while dodging obstacles. It becomes second nature.

Absorbing Bumps

Find a partner of similar size and weight to practice with. Ride around a short, traffic-free course side by side at a steady speed. Begin bumping elbows and shoulders gently, looking straight ahead. Keep your bike close to vertical as you lean into

the other rider. The motion is similar to the steering technique—
the bike stays upright, and you move over it. Steer rather than
turn away from the other cyclist, if you need to. Stay as relaxed
as possible and keep your elbows bent. I have my coaches ride
alongside the campers and perform an elbow check, lightly striking an arm to make sure the rider can absorb it without veering.
You get used to it.

Avoiding Obstacles

Another drill I recommend is "plungering," so named because I use the rubber portions of toilet plungers as obstacles.
Here's how it works. I place ten plungers in a line on a traffic-
free road, about 10 feet apart. Your goal is to head straight for
the line of plungers and move your bike quickly around them,
first to one side and then to the other, as if slaloming. The key is
to keep your body over the plungers while moving the bike underneath you. There's also two-up and three-up plungering, where
you must avoid the obstacles while one or two riders bump and
lean into you. (See the photo on page 95.)

Of course, you needn't use plungers. You can just pick a spot
in the road, such as a manhole cover, and dodge it. Put your nose
right over the obstacle and move your bike underneath you to
get around it.

You can also combine plungers with the cul-de-sac drill to
become comfortable cornering with others. Place the plungers in
a concentric circle about 5 feet inside the boundary of the cul-
de-sac. Complete the drill as described previously, but this time
do it with another rider at your side.

Discipline 3:
Touching Wheels

Overlapping and touching wheels is something you should
avoid at all costs. That's what makes this drill so difficult—you
must purposefully put yourself in a dangerous position. But it's
worth it. The key is to steer, not lean and turn, once contact is
made. If you lean, your center of gravity will be off, and you'll
crash.

To improve balance and bike handling, coach Mike Walden recommends "three-up plungering."

Have a partner ride in front of you, straight and steady. Overlap wheels just an inch or so and attempt to tap your partner's rear wheel by steering your front into it. Then immediately steer away, but don't overcorrect, which is one of the most common causes of crashes in this situation. Repeat from the other side. Eventually you'll learn how much steering is required to escape this dangerous situation.

Discipline 4:
Paceline Riding

A paceline isn't just for racers. It's the most efficient way to ride in a small group, no matter what the speed. In fact, you'll reap an energy savings of as much as 30 percent by using one. And it's fun. But you have to do it all the time and get so you can sit on a wheel without burning nervous energy. For my riders, paceline riding is as automatic as breathing.

The Anatomy of a Paceline

A paceline is actually two groups side by side. The faster one is the advance line. Riders reaching the front continue pedaling and immediately swing into the slower relief line. Riders reaching the back of the relief line accelerate and join the advance line, in a circular movement. (See the illustration on the opposite page.)

In training, the advance line should be on the left. This is because some riders tend to swing wide after reaching the front. With the advance line on the right, this can put them in traffic, or worse, into the opposing lane. Of course, if you have a closed road, you should let the wind dictate the direction of the rotation. The advance line should be on the sheltered (leeward) side.

Novices should use an open paceline in which riders in the relief line leave a bike length between themselves. This prevents a common error. In switching to the advance line, some riders panic, accelerate too hard, and end up between the lines. This is a dangerous spot because there's no escape route.

Pointers on Pacelines

Here are other points to remember.

- Look at nothing, but see everything. Use your peripheral vision and keep your head up. Don't stare at the wheel in front or the back of someone's head.
- When you reach the front, pedal harder but not faster. Resist the temptation to jump. When in the second posi-

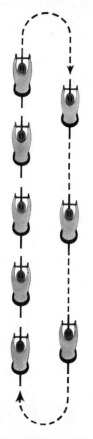

The movement in this paceline drill is circular, as riders in the advance line (left) turn off the front into the relief line.

tion, note your speed and maintain it when pulling through.

- Turn off the front and steer onto the back. You turn off the front because it's the easiest thing to do, and you'll probably be tired. But you steer to join the advance line. This way, if you touch wheels, you won't crash. You just pull the bike back underneath you. If you're turning (leaning) in this situation, you're going down.

- Adjust your speed gradually. Don't jump to fill a gap because it will affect the rhythm of the group. On the other hand, if you must slow, feather your brakes and continue pedaling.
- Eat and drink while in the relief line. It's slower and requires less concentration.

Discipline 5:
Climbing Efficiently

The most common climbing error is waiting too long before shifting. This includes downshifting and upshifting. Adjust your cadence when the hill steepens as well as when it flattens. This is the fastest, most efficient way.

Most hills have three segments: the approach, the climb, and a somewhat level portion at the crest. I'll use some hypothetical cadences to describe the proper technique, but you must discover your most efficient range.

Let's say you're pedaling at 90 rpm on the flats. Once you're into the hill's approach it drops to 87. You should immediately downshift and increase your cadence to say, 100—an artificially high number. Once you're into the climb it will begin to drop again. When it gets down to about 90, shift to a lower gear to increase cadence, and so on, as the hill steepens. The key is to shift early, avoid lactic acid buildup, and preserve your legs.

When the hill begins to level, your cadence will rise to say, 92. Immediately slam on more gear. Go to an artificially low cadence, say 80. At the same time, switch to a more powerful pedaling technique by dropping your heels. Stand if necessary to get on top of the gear. Shift up several more times as the hill continues to flatten.

Once you crest the climb, don't coast. Pedal down the other side to work out any lactic acid.

Discipline 6:
Sprinting

One of my rules is never accelerate in undisturbed air. Nowhere is this more important than in sprinting. Whether you're racing or just doing town-line sprints with your clubmates, you should practice the skill of drafting and coming off someone's wheel.

Switch and Finish

I use a drill called the switch and finish. Find a partner and establish a finish line on a low-traffic road. With about half a mile to go, one rider accelerates to 23 to 25 mph, and the other drafts. With 200 meters to go the second rider backs off about a bike length, then accelerates in the first rider's slipstream and sling-shots past. Time the jump so that a bike throw is required at the line to win. Switch positions and repeat.

What does this teach you? Most important, your initial acceleration should occur in the slipstream, behind the other rider, not by jumping directly into the wind. It also accustoms you to the feel of sprinting in close quarters.

Counterattack

In a real sprint, sometimes a rider will try to hook you by moving abruptly sideways. This leaves you no choice but to put your shoulder into that person and keep going. In 99 out of 100 instances, you're going to knock that guy down. This is because your bike is upright and safe, while the other person's is at a critical lean angle.

Sound ruthless? Remember that cycling is a game, and you must play it to the limit of the rules. If I catch one of my riders knocking someone down deliberately, I come down hard on that person. On the other hand, if someone hooks my rider and he or she backs off, I come down on the person for that, too. That's the way the game is played.

21 MAKING YOUR WEAK POINTS STRONG

Although my training program is gradual and systematic, during spring you should be just piling on the miles. Do longer and longer rides at faster and faster speeds. Build on what you have. Add speed, then add endurance. Add more speed, then add more endurance.

Are You a Recreational Rider or a Racer?

How much you do depends on your goals. Are you a fast recreational rider and not a racer? I have no argument with that. Maybe you're satisfied with your fitness, and you're thinking: "Hey, Mike, I don't want to get up and bleed on Sunday mornings." Well, that's good enough for me. Just keep riding.

On the other hand, maybe you have a specific goal such as a fast century or race. If so, there are workouts you can do to fine-tune your fitness.

But first, a note for riders older than 30 who have a reasonable mileage base. Because you probably need to squeeze your cycling around a job and family, I recommend you go as hard as you can, as long as you can, and as often as you can. Within reason, it's hard to hurt mature riders. I call this pressure training. I want you in the cooker. You only have so much time, so go right to your capacity. De-emphasize technical training and just do it.

But if you're younger or not sufficiently fit, you have to be careful. If you get an injury, it could become chronic. So continued gradual development and skill work are the rules for such riders.

Negative Coaching

Sound bad? It's not. I use negative coaching all the time and you should, too. It simply means analyzing weaknesses and working to eliminate them. It's a particularly valuable approach in the spring and early summer.

When I work with riders, I don't try to remedy a bunch of things at once. I'm constantly looking at my cyclists and saying, "What can I do to make this person better?" I wait for them to make mistakes, and then I correct them. I don't create cookie-cutter athletes.

For instance, you might always be lagging in the hills. If so, obviously you need to work on your climbing skills. Or perhaps you're one of the fastest cyclists at the beginning of a ride, but you fade after 50 miles. You need to work on endurance or experiment with on-bike nutrition. Or maybe you can ride at a steady pace all day but have trouble responding to changes in tempo. The solution for this is speedwork. And if you suffer in time trials or fast flatland riding, you need power training.

Skill-Building Workouts

I'll detail specific workouts to develop all of these skills. Pick your chief weakness and substitute my drill for one of the two interval sessions you should be doing weekly.

Before I describe the workouts, I'll mention one other aid that's invaluable at any time of year: video analysis. I constantly use it at my school. It's particularly beneficial if you don't have a coach because it enables you to be your own teacher. You can't analyze your pedal stroke by looking in the mirror. You have to watch yourself riding. Have someone film you in a variety of situations to diagnose climbing, cornering, sprinting, bike position, and other important skills. Use the previous chapters to make sure you're doing each one correctly.

Improving Climbing

In chapter 20, I examined proper climbing technique, which basically involves shifting before you need to. Here's a way to practice the skill and improve fitness at the same time.

I like to use two ¼-mile-long ascents with a valley in between. This way you can work both sides. In the middle of each hill I mark a distance of about 100 yards. Start by going to the bottom and almost stopping. Then begin ascending, spinning in a comfortable gear while seated. When you reach the start of the 100-yard section, shift to a higher gear, stand, and accelerate. (If you were attending my camp, here's where I'd be giving you a hard time.) Once you get on top of this gear, switch to the next higher one (smaller cog), and so on, until the end of the marked area. Then sit and try to maintain your speed to the top. (See the illustration on page 102.)

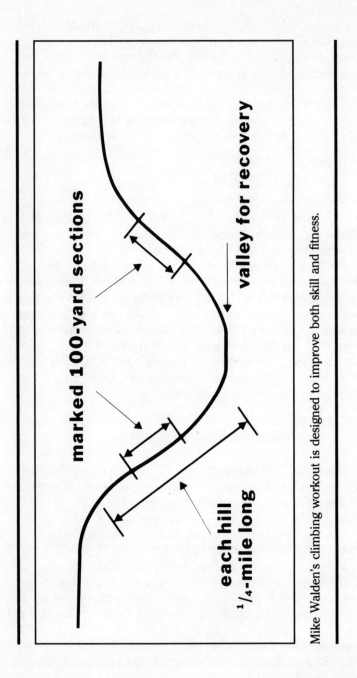

Mike Walden's climbing workout is designed to improve both skill and fitness.

Afterward, turn around and pedal easily to the bottom. Come to a near-stop, then ascend the other hill the same way. The idea is to go back and forth until you can't make it anymore. When you don't recover at the bottom, the workout is over.

Building Power

I have a specific way to build power, such as for time trials. The key is to ride for short periods or do intervals at faster than your target speed. This enables you to ride longer at a slightly slower pace—the pace you hope to maintain in the event.

Here's an analogy. I often tell people that there's not a rider in the world who can complete 200 meters at full speed. There isn't. But there are plenty of sprinters who can go 200 meters at 99 percent of max. So what you have to do is train at a speed that's greater than you can ever maintain for the chosen distance and hope that eventually you can extend it. In the process, this regimen improves your recovery rate. This is what training is all about: making your body adapt to the task at hand.

Let's say you want to do a 40-kilometer time trial at 25 mph. Chances are you can go 28 mph for half a mile. Do this in training, recover, then repeat until you can't maintain it. Eventually, you'll be able to do almost the full distance—in intervals—at a speed greater than you hope to maintain for the event. Then you'll find that you can attain your goal pace on the big day.

Increasing Endurance

You don't build endurance just by riding miles. Sure, long rides are valuable, but there's a better way. It's similar to the regimen used for building power. The key is to increase speed, then distance, then add more speed, and more distance.

First, decide what speed you want to maintain. Let's say your goal is to average 16 mph for a century. In training, ride 18 mph until you can't do it anymore. Don't slow. If you do, stop and get off the bike until you're rested. Then get back on and ride 18 mph, and so on.

The idea is to bring the intensity up, then the distance. Don't take your training to the endurance limit, take it to the speed limit. This way, when you're actually doing the event, you're staying away from the capacity of the muscles.

Getting Faster

There are lots of ways to build speed. Be creative. You could establish a relatively traffic-free course that's about four blocks around. Sprint one side as hard as possible, recover completely on the second side, then sprint the third. Do some against the wind and some with the wind.

Or, if you're cycling in a group, assign lead-out riders. One guy starts the first sprint, another the second, and so on. Each time, the rest of the field tries to come around that person. A coach can make it even better by telling someone to screw it up and go at an inopportune moment. This works well because it simulates competition. Bike racing never goes smoothly.

Sometimes I have my riders work on the initial jump. The idea is to use a relatively big gear and start from a slow speed. You have to get both feet into it. Don't be a one-legged pedaler. Push with one while pulling with the other, and push and pull with your arms in opposition to your legs. Hold your body stiff and pull the bike and pedals up against each foot. Too many riders pull their bodies over the bike instead.

Tapering

Here's another of my adages: "No pain, no gain, but too much pain and it's all in vain." This means resting the week before an important event. Don't even get close to being tired. Of course, this doesn't imply that you shouldn't ride. Instead, cut way down on endurance and concentrate on speed, which should be slightly faster than what you hope to maintain in the event. Here's another way to think of it: You want to come into the event as fresh as possible but with speed in hand.

Keep in mind, however, that this assumes you're in shape. If not, you might as well train through the event. Use it to improve fitness.

The last few days are crucial. If your event is on Sunday, then Friday should be an easy day. Ride to a friend's house or use the bike for transportation. Do whatever you feel like doing, but don't go fast or hard.

The day before an event is different. Briefly simulate what you hope to do in your target ride or race. For instance, if it's a century or time trial, spend some time at goal pace or faster. For a criterium, do some full-on sprints that are 100 meters long rather than the normal 200. If you're doing a road race, climb a few short hills very fast. The idea is to do what you'll be doing in the event, but less of it. Bring your level up slightly, but avoid getting tired.

Finding Your Efficient Cadence

Here's something you should incorporate into your riding. To me, cadence is more than just pedal speed in revolutions per minute. I define it as rpm times pedal pressure. I also call it energy burn rate. Everyone has an ideal cadence, and it's their most efficient way to use energy. The goal is to stay as close to it as you can while handling as big a gear as you can.

A cadence test. I have a test that will allow you to discover your ideal cadence and gear at different speeds. You'll need a flat course, a cyclecomputer with speed and cadence functions, and a heart rate monitor.

1. Ride in about an 83-inch gear (52 × 17 teeth) at 22 mph. Record your cadence and heart rate after it stabilizes. Recover completely.
2. Use the same course, distance and speed, but this time shift to the next higher gear (e.g., 52 × 16). Record heart rate and cadence, then recover.
3. Repeat number 2.
4. Repeat number 1.

To check validity, reverse the order two days later. Do step number 2, then number 1, then number 1 again, and number 2 again.

Two days later, repeat the process at a slightly higher speed of, say, 24 mph.

Analyze the numbers to determine your optimum cadence and gear at each speed. You'll find them by looking for the lowest

Ideal Cadence/Gear at 22 mph

Gear (in.)	Speed (mph)	Cadence (rpm)	Heart Rate (bpm)
Trial No. 1			
83	22	90	156–57
88	22	85	150–52*
88	22	85	154–55*
83	22	90	157–58
Trial No. 2			
88	22	85	152–53*
83	22	90	158–60
83	22	90	159–61
88	22	85	154–55*

* Lowest heart rate in both trials occurred when using larger (88-inch) gear.

heart rate at each of the speeds. For instance, you may note that for a speed of 22 mph, you're more efficient at 85 rpm (52 × 16) rather than 90 rpm (52 × 17). Consequently, strive to use this cadence and gear at that speed.

Obviously, you can't test and memorize the correct gear for every speed. However, in general, strive to become familiar with cadence as it relates to your physiology. Select gears that make you efficient and result in the lowest heart rate. (See the table above.) This way, by constantly studying yourself and your performance, you'll become your own best coach. Then you can concentrate on playing the game of cycling.

22 GETTING THE MOST FROM OFF-SEASON TRAINING

Fall is your rest period, so enjoy it. From October through December you shouldn't stress your system, at least not compared to what you've been doing in season. This doesn't mean you should sit on the couch.

Staying in Shape

I'm a big advocate of cross-training—if it's done right. Here's my overriding rule: Don't do anything with your legs that doesn't mimic the motion of riding a bike. This means no weight training. It doesn't teach your muscles to fire in a sequence that's similar to cycling. Not even close.

The activity also has to be low impact. Consequently, I don't like running. It causes too many injuries. Cyclocross and mountain biking are great, but be careful because you can get injured in these sports, too. Cross-country skiing is also good.

My Schwinn Wolverine Sports Club is known for its emphasis on speed skating. It's an excellent, low-impact form of cross-training that has proven successful with cyclists. When you force the blade into the ice you're using almost the same muscles as you do when cycling. And you're burning energy at a high rate. Of course, not everyone can locate skating facilities or coaching expertise. So one of the other major cross-training methods I use is hill walking. You should also include upper-body work such as hitting a speed bag (see page 111).

No matter what activities you choose, you must maintain contact with your road bike, primarily by riding a fixed gear. You would shortchange yourself for the coming season if you just did cyclocross all winter and never worked on the disciplines of steering, sprinting, and the like. Remember that any cross-training method involves a compromise. You'll gain something in one area, but you'll lose something in another. You need to come up with an equation that works for you.

The off-season is also a good time to get back to basics. If you haven't done so already, correct flaws in position (see chapter 19) and establish your ideal cadence and gears through the test I've designed in chapter 21 (see pages 105–106).

Capillary Development

I divide the off-season into periods for capillary development and muscle development. The first is a low-intensity program that supplies tremendous benefits later in the year, but it requires patience and self-restraint.

It involves increasing the capacity of your capillaries. A piece of veal from a calf has a pale look because it transported very little blood. Conversely, a piece of beef from a cow that's been in the field a few years is deep purple from carrying so much blood. The elasticity of the capillaries has been increased by low-intensity exercise. This same phenomenon can occur with humans.

Low-Intensity Riding

To do it properly, I recommend about 200 hours of work (or at least one month of steady riding). Some of this can be done off the bike through activities such as walking, but the best way is fixed-gear riding at a heart rate of no more than two-thirds your capacity (generally, less than 135 beats per minute). While you're doing this, you can practice cornering and all your other skills, so the time isn't wasted. Just play on the bike and keep track of your hours.

But here's the catch. If you go hard before accumulating the correct amount of low-intensity hours, you've ruined all that capillary work. Lactic acid gets pushed through the capillary cells and blows them up. You feel this as a burning sensation. When they heal, they do so at a smaller size. On the other hand, if you've done the requisite number of hours, the cells have grown permanently larger and can transport more oxygenated blood.

So the biggest problem is restraining yourself. Let's say you're riding this way for a month, and you're feeling great. So you say, "I'll think I'll try a sprint," or "I'll chase down that cyclist up the road." You do, and suddenly you've blown a month's work. You'll have some residual benefits, but they'll be nowhere near as much as if you had behaved yourself.

Muscle Building

Once you've completed the capillary phase, start muscle development. This is my version of weight training. It includes rigorous cross-training such as skating, cross-country skiing, or the hill walking regimen described later. It also involves sprint training on the bike three times per week, with three sprints included in each session. The key is that the volume is reduced. Instead of a normal 200-meter sprint, limit it to 60 to 80 meters.

Using a Fixed Gear

I like my athletes to ride at least 1,000 miles in a fixed gear before doing the demanding training that starts in the spring. This can encompass both the capillary and muscle development periods. It'll benefit your pedal stroke tremendously.

You can install a fixed gear on your road bike, or better, convert a beater bike for the purpose. If possible, select the gear based on your ideal cadence test for the speed at which you'll be riding. In general, use one that will allow you to complete most rides in your area at 90 rpm or more without overtaxing your knees. Typically, this is a 70- to 90-inch gear. If you have a 42-tooth small chainring, combine it with a cog that has 13, 14, 15, or 16 teeth. Err on the side of a lower rather than higher gear. A shop can sell you a cog and lockring that will screw onto your hub, or you can have an old freewheel spot-welded in several places to eliminate the ratcheting feature. This last option allows you to choose among the cogs. I recommend using a track chain, which has a wider, ⅛-inch pitch. It's less flexible and not as likely to derail. Remove the rear derailleur and cable. Shorten the chain and adjust wheel position so there's about ½ inch of vertical play in the middle of the chain.

Hill Walking

A lot of riders don't believe in walking to the corner store, much less doing it for conditioning. But I recommend easy, flat walks year-round to promote recovery after rides and help digestion after meals. As a cross-training method, I advocate hill walking, done as hard and fast as possible. You can get a dynamite workout and develop cycling muscles at the same time.

Start with a flat, 1-mile warm-up and some stretching exercises. The best type of hill is grass covered and shaped like an inverted bowl. This way you can climb it at an angle from each side. (See the illustration on page 110.) Otherwise, if you're using

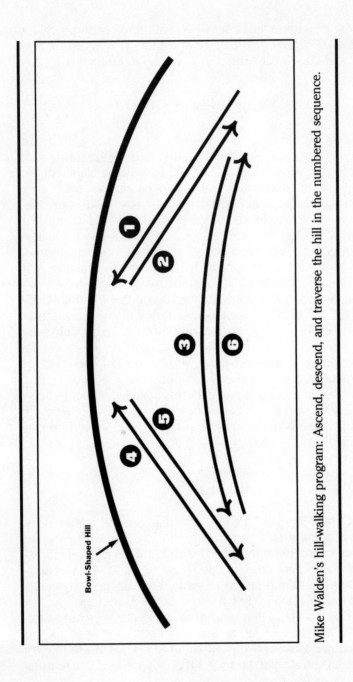

Mike Walden's hill-walking program: Ascend, descend, and traverse the hill in the numbered sequence.

a ridge, simply traverse it at a 45-degree angle. Take about 40 seconds to make the ascent. Take the longest stride possible and keep your feet parallel, just like when you're pedaling. Doing so slightly twists the ankles, knees, and hips, which helps build strength and protects you from injury. Then turn around and come down the same way, taking as long as you like. Next, walk along the base (but not on the flat), do the other side of the bowl, and so on. Limit the workout to about an hour, three times per week. Later, add hand weights.

Using a Speed Bag

One of the biggest things that bike riders lack is coordination between their hands and feet. They're clumsy. So I recommend off-season activities such as skipping rope or swimming. But my favorite is to work out with a lightweight speed bag hung from the ceiling.

What has punching a bag got to do with cycling? Plenty. It helps reaction time and benefits bike handling. When I introduce riders to my cul-de-sac drill (chapter 20), they often have trouble shifting their weight back and forth over the bike. The coordination just isn't there. In general, cycling doesn't demand fast reflexes. But in an emergency, or during sprints or fast cornering, you have to be quick. Hitting a speed bag helps develop this. It also accustoms your arms and chest muscles to absorbing shock. This is good for riding on rough roads or tolerating bumps from other cyclists.

You can often find a speed bag at a YMCA. Otherwise, buy the biggest inflatable model you can. Keep in mind that this is different from a tall, heavy, body bag. You're not trying to build power.

To set the height, bend over as if you were riding on the handlebar drops. Stand up, bringing your arms with you in the position they were in. Put the bulbous part of the bag where your hands are, but not so high that you strike it with the heels of your hands.

It's always amusing to watch bike riders hit a bag for the first time. Their hands are moving, but in a way that's seemingly unconnected to the rest of their bodies. They only have coordination in their legs. On the other hand, my cyclists hit the bag with the grace of dancers.

Don't punch it like a boxer, who jabs with the hand and forearm. Keep your elbow aligned with your fist, so the energy is transferred through your arm, back, and legs. And don't look directly at the bag. This way, you'll develop your peripheral vision. If possible, do speed-bag workouts for half an hour three times per week.

Remember that upper-body exercises can also be what I call supplemental training. That is, they can be done at a low intensity throughout the year, not just in the off-season. This will help keep your torso and arms in shape when your main emphasis switches to the bike.

◻ CREDITS

The information in this book was drawn from these and other articles in *Bicycling* Magazine.

"The First Step to Powerful Riding" Geoff Drake, "Perfect Positions," March 1990.

"Aerodynamics Give Fast Results" Geoff Drake, "Aero Answers," May 1990.

"Alexi Grewal on Seated Climbing" Geoff Drake, "Alexi Grewal On: Seated Climbing," December 1990.

"Davis Phinney on Out-of-Saddle Climbing" Geoff Drake, "Davis Phinney On: Out-of-Saddle Climbing," July 1991.

"Steve Bauer on Full-Tuck Descending" Geoff Drake, "Steve Bauer On: Full-Tuck Descending," January/February 1991.

"Frankie Andreu on Pack Riding" Geoff Drake, "Frankie Andreu On: Pack Riding," March 1991.

"Brian Walton on Paceline Riding" Geoff Drake, "Brian Walton On: Paceline Riding," May 1991.

"Ron Kiefel on Time Trialing" Geoff Drake, "Ron Kiefel On: Time Trialing," November 1990.

"Chris Kostman on Long-Distance Cycling" Chris Kostman, "The Double Century," April 1989.

"Finding a Cadence for Efficient Pedaling" Steve Johnson, Ph.D., "Cadence," April 1989.

"The Revealing Story behind Your VO₂ Max" Steve Johnson, Ph.D., "VO₂ Max," January/February 1989.

"Target Heart Rate: The Point at Which Fitness Begins" Steve Johnson, Ph.D., "Target Heart Rate," July 1989.

"What's at the Anaerobic Threshold?" Steve Johnson, Ph.D., "Anaerobic Threshold," March 1989.

"Overtraining: The Disease of Excellence" Connie Carpenter Phinney, "Overtraining," August 1988.

"A No-Nonsense Guide to Cycling Nutrition" Virginia DeMoss, "Eater's Digest," March 1991.

"How to Eat to Beat 'The Bonk' " Steve Johnson, Ph.D., "Bonk," August 1989; Ellen Coleman, M.S., R.D., "Eating for Endurance," May 1989.

"What Racers Really Eat for Power" Tim Blumenthal and Geoff Drake, "Mean Cuisine," November 1990.

"Mike Walden's Proven Year-Round Program" Geoff Drake, "Walden's Way," June 1991.

"The Essential Elements of Better Training" Geoff Drake, "Walden's Way," June 1991.

"The Key Disciplines of Bike Handling" Geoff Drake, "Walden's Way: Part II," July 1991.

"Making Your Weak Points Strong" Geoff Drake, "Walden's Way: Part III," August 1991.

"Getting the Most from Off-Season Training" Geoff Drake, "Walden's Way: Part IV," November 1991.

Photographs

Page 4: Mitch Mandel/Rodale Stock Images
Page 11: Angelo Caggiano/Rodale Stock Images
Page 18: Karen Schulenberg
Page 22: Mike Shaw
Page 27: Yann Guichaoua/Vandystadt Allsport USA
Page 32: Graham Watson
Page 36: Yann Guichaoua/Vandystadt Allsport USA
Page 81: Chris Stickney

Page 92: David Madison
Page 95: David Madison

Illustrations

Page 97: Kathi Ember
Page 102: Courtesy of *Bicycling* Magazine
Page 110: Courtesy of *Bicycling* Magazine